VOICELESS

by
Mathias Wallace

The contents of this work, including, but not limited to, the accuracy of events, people, and places depicted; opinions expressed; permission to use previously published materials included; and any advice given or actions advocated are solely the responsibility of the author, who assumes all liability for said work and indemnifies the publisher against any claims stemming from publication of the work.

All Rights Reserved
Copyright © 2019 by Mathias Wallace

No part of this book may be reproduced or transmitted, downloaded, distributed, reverse engineered, or stored in or introduced into any information storage and retrieval system, in any form or by any means, including photocopying and recording, whether electronic or mechanical, now known or hereinafter invented without permission in writing from the publisher.

Dorrance Publishing Co
585 Alpha Drive
Pittsburgh, PA 15238
Visit our website at *www.dorrancebookstore.com*

ISBN: 978-1-6442-6211-5
eISBN 978-1-6442-6393-8

VOICELESS

Chapter One

THE TRUTH IS

"Choose! Choose right now, Jeremiah! You can go upstairs, pack your bags, and come with mommy or you can get dressed, go to school and stay here." Five-year-old Jeremiah stood there motionless and muted. As he stood there confused and dazed he began to ponder the options and the consequences for each decision. His young mind contemplated the options as he balanced himself on the second step of the stairway leading up to bedrooms on the second level of the apartment. Stricken with fear, Jeremiah suddenly realized this was not a case of choosing whether to go to school versus a field trip with his mother, but rather he was being asked to choose between staying in the city with his father or leaving for the countryside with his mother and two younger siblings.

Jeremiah hadn't realized the length of time taken to make up his decision; his brother Troy and sister Catherine were already placed in their aunt Lucille's car which was waiting outside. Jeremiah knew his life would never be the same. There, in the deep depths of his mind, Jeremiah sunk into a place where nothing else existed, paralyzed by shock and puzzled by the outcome of his day as it started with such promise.

Jeremiah wasn't like many children; he loved going to school and learning. He didn't know then that his love for academics would have a profound impact on his life. Some may say school was his anchor in life. When he jumped out of bed earlier that morning, he was glowing with joy and oozing excitement out of his ears, as it was finally time to get prepared for school and spend the day learning and having fun with his friends. Instead, he was now standing in the stairway, voiceless. Unable to verbally reply to his mom, with immense unwillingness to declare one parent over the other, Jeremiah turned around and walked upstairs to pack.

How long is the trip? Where are we going? How much do I pack? When are we coming back? We are coming back, right? Right? Jeremiah couldn't find the strength, courage, or the words to ask those questions of his dear mother. How could he, after the look of death his mother gave him while she delivered her ultimatum. Gloria, a woman of strong will, was known for not allowing kids to sass her.

Therefore, any child, especially one of her own, knew better than to question her. Gloria was short, but her mighty demeanor gave her the appearance of a giant in Jeremiah's eyes. Glaring at what appeared to be an endless row of trees, Jeremiah realized he was no longer near the place he once called home in the vibrant city. Unfortunately, this wouldn't be the last time Jeremiah would be suppressed into a motionless state and verbally incapacitated, or in other words, voiceless.

Overwhelmed with emotions he'd never experienced before, Jeremiah somehow managed to maintain his composure without upsetting his mother Gloria with his subsequent confusion with this current life change. His siblings, Troy and Catherine, were far too young to understand how their life had shifted, so they played in the backseat of Lucille's car as if life was peachy. The twins played tug-of-war in their car seats. Jeremiah couldn't help but ponder on the thoughts of his father Zander and what role his father would play in their lives.

As the journey continued to this unknown destination, poor little Jeremiah attempted to internalize the fact that the family he once adored no longer existed. He sat in the back seat observing his surroundings, as no one mentioned his father's name during this torturous ride as piece by piece the life he once knew was stripped away. Like many poor families of the African American community growing up in the southeast, the father played a significant role for his family, and Jeremiah was devastated by his new reality. What can you do in this situation? How can a child change the outcome of such a sensitive and yet severe life change?

Jeremiah was Zander's biggest fan and greatest admirer! A few Saturdays of each month, Zander would take his son through the city for a routine trip. Jeremiah would awake from his bed bursting with energy and elated because he knew he was moments away from the regular adventure with his father. As they walked through the city, Jeremiah, who was only about three feet tall, did his best to keep up with his father, who stood 6'3" tall. From time to time, Zander would lift Jeremiah high into the sky to make him feel invincible. "Here we go again, son," Zander would say before thrusting him into the air again.

Jeremiah's favorite moment was when Zander would place him on his shoulders as they walked throughout the city. "I feel as though I'm on top of the world, Dad," Jeremiah stated to his father.

"That's because you are, my son!" Empowered by the love and support of his father, Jeremiah lifted his head in complete confidence as they walked into the bright white building. In this building, most people had white strokes of wisdom in their hair as they laid on the fluffy white bed connected to tubes with doctors standing over them. The people in this open floor space loved to see Jeremiah walk through the facility with his father. They all wanted to meet and greet and share their stories, or sometimes just their love of children.

Finally, Zander was called, and the doctor laid him across the bed and asked a series of questions. Jeremiah stood there bravely as he was offered snacks while his father completed the questionnaire. After the questioning session was complete, Jeremiah watched as they connected the same tubes to his father's arm that he ascertained on the other strangers in the room. Wrapped in a state of bewilderment, Jeremiah watched as the red lava flowed from his father's arm through the tube and into the clear bag hanging above his head. Perplexed by this moment, he stood there concerned, and Zander grabbed Jeremiah's hand as he watched fear fill the eyes of his angelic son. The procedure didn't last long, and shortly afterward, Zander and Jeremiah signed the final paperwork, waved goodbye to the elders in the room, and proceeded out the door as Zander stuffed the green men into his pocket.

Zander led his son next door to the cafe were all participants flowed shortly after the procedure. Jeremiah had always been a big fan of food, and he was the only one of the younger kids who was taken off children vitamins because he simply ate too much. He wasn't shy in the kitchen. The fear and worry that once filled his heart was soon overtaken by the joy which filled his body as the sensors in his nose were delighted by the aroma of the food. Everyone seemed to be so cheerful and full of life. Such humility filled this room on every visit, as if everyone was equal and in tune, together. Smiles covered the faces of those sitting and serving in this room, and it completely captivated Jeremiah.

The walk back home was always dreadful for Jeremiah, as he knew the adventure with his father was coming to an end. He took advantage of every moment to be lifted into the sky by his father on the way back home. Although Jeremiah was smart and extremely observant for his age, he didn't realize the true dynamics of their lifestyle or how his mother and father struggled daily at this point in his life. However, this would all change shortly for Jeremiah.

"Here we are," said Lucille as they finally arrived at their destination. Lucille was a proud Southern Belle and Christian woman. She held her nose high in the air as she knew certain aspects of her life were much better than others, including her immediate family. Jeremiah glanced past the one-level family home with blue trimming into the backyard where a black fifty-pound dog stood starring back at him. Fixated on the dog, Jeremiah didn't notice the two girls and one little boy standing in the doorway awaiting their arrival. *These are your cousins April, Rebecca, and Jonathan.* April was the youngest of the three and appeared to be quite shy. Rebecca was taller than April but was thinner, with hair down to her back, meanwhile Troy was a scrawny and tall fella who stood there with a distant look on his face.

Days passed, and young Jeremiah quickly realized this nightmare was his new reality and that there was nothing he could do about it except adapt to the new environment. Behind Lucille's brick home was a single-wide mobile home for Gloria and her three younger kids while Aunt Lucille and the three cousins lived in the house. Jeremiah had never seen a mobile home in the projects of the inner city. Electricity and water were all connected to the brick home, so the mobile home was not self-sufficient.

Being in the Deep South, Jeremiah and his family experienced hot summer days and cold winter nights as they did their best to survive with a box fan and floor heater. Gloria was a woman who knew how to make the best out of any situation. She quickly sectioned off the trailer so that the heat or cool air would remain consistent in at least one portion of the house so that her kids could live more comfortably. Although Gloria was doing her best to provide for her kids, Jeremiah, Troy, and Catherine struggled with the cold water during bath time, as the water was filtered from the bathroom window through a water hose. The three siblings would bundle together on those cold winter nights to fight the chills spreading over their tiny bodies. Jeremiah oftentimes found himself outside at different times of the day reconnecting the orange and black cords outside of the trailer because Boxer, the dog, frequently untangled them. He didn't notice at first, but Jeremiah began to watch as his mom would disappear in the back section of the trailer from time to time.

During the day, the three siblings would find any excuse to enter the brick home to spend time with their cousins. They enjoyed the time spent with the newly discovered relatives, and not only because the house was always set at a comfortable temperature and food was throughout the kitchen, but because playing with other kids distracted Jeremiah from the true hardships waiting at their new home. Many warm and sunny summer days were spent climbing the trees in Lucille's yard which overflowed with berries. Red berries and blackberries everywhere! Giggles and screams filled the air as the cousins indulged in the abundance of berries.

Catherine thought she was sneaky as she picked the berries that had already fallen to the ground. "Put that down," yelled Troy, standing seven feet to her right with a mouth full of berries. Jeremiah, Rebecca, and April, being the oldest of the cousins, aside from Jonathan, all laughed hysterically as Catherine dropped her berries. Jonathan never spent much time outside with the rest of the kids. He preferred staying in his room, listening to music, and playing his guitar. April liked to have fun, but she never stuck around for too long. One minute all the kids would be out playing freeze tag, and before you knew it, April was nowhere to be found. She was a silly little character, and her presence was always enjoyed, as her infectious laugh possessed you and forced participation in laughter at her corny jokes. There was something special about the bond between cousins. They enjoyed many summer days of being young, wild, and free.

Chapter Two

THE SHIFT

Many moons passed, and the cousins grew closer and closer to one another even though their living conditions were significantly different. Jeremiah and his sibling would ask if they could sleep over with April and Rebecca, although they only lived fifty feet away in the house with their aunt Lucille. After a few overnight stays, Jeremiah and the others quickly learned there were many versions of their dear aunt. Over time, the kids began to see a different side of Lucille when visiting for extended periods of time.

"Stop tracking in my house," a loud, robust voice would yell from the back of the house. No matter how soft the little children tried to walk down the halls, Lucille with the hearing capabilities of a bat could always catch them. "Quick making all of that ruckus," the voice would yell again after hearing snickering travel the hallway and into her room. Rebecca, Jeremiah, April, Troy, and Catherine would all drop to the floor and cover their mouths to prevent more laughter from spilling out. "Shhhhh," said April in a sudden panic! Of the crew, April hated getting into trouble the worst. Rebecca reached up to pull the string on the lamp. The room instantly went dark, and little Catherine belched a high-pitched scream at the top of her lungs. "What's wrong with you?" asked Jeremiah. He reached for her in distress and tried to comfort her quickly before their aunt entered the room.

Rebecca and April shared a room directly across from their aunt, and Jonathan's room was down the hall. The girls had twin beds on opposite sides of the bedroom and an elaborate display of posters and pictures on the walls. Rebecca and April always kept their room spotless with every barbie doll, stuffed animal, and decorative pillow positioned perfectly. I guess you could say they were trained by the best, Aunt Lucille. She had all the furniture in the living room covered in plastic because she didn't want guests transferring dirt onto her stylish sofa set. This beautiful white tiger hung above the gorgeous oak table, and little ornaments were displayed aesthetically throughout to the entertainment room. Family pictures covered the tables and the walls. Jeremiah and his siblings would often ask questions, as none of the photos were familiar to them.

When the group of cousins were not traveling through time as they gazed through photo albums, playing in the room, or eating mouthfuls of berries, they spent many afternoons traversing the streets through their neighborhood. The cousins avoided certain streets, as many neighbors had vicious dogs that roamed freely. Nothing says you're living the country life like being chased by one or more dogs while simply taking a gentle stroll. Jeremiah was the fastest runner of them all, but oftentimes found himself pulling Troy alone, as he was three years younger and couldn't keep up as well as Rebecca. April hardly ever joined the spontaneous walks through the neighborhood, but that worked out perfectly because Catherine enjoyed having some distance from her twin, so they stayed back home. Most trips led the cousins to the local corner store to purchase snacks. Their mouths filled with saliva as they stuffed their plastic bags with the best chewy candy in the world! "Don't get all of the blue ones," yelled Troy, as blue was his favorite color.

Spending time enjoying the simple things in life brought so much joy to the young group of cousins, from teaching each other how to draw, playing hide and seek, and taking the dog for walks through the woods which surrounded their property. Over time, it appeared Jeremiah and his siblings were spending a little too much time at their Aunt Lucille's house. It was written all over her face.

Although she was a respected Southern Belle, her level of kindness often came with a tolerance cap. Lucille was an educated woman with a degree in the business field, and she worked at the local university in their hometown. Meanwhile, Gloria had a degree in the medical field and had finally secured a job at the community nursing home. She spent most of her time working and reconnecting with long lost relatives and close friends in the area since she mostly grew up there in the small town. While she explored the town, Jeremiah was tasked with keeping an eye on his siblings until his mother returned. Being so young, there was only so much Jeremiah knew about taking care of kids, but this was different because it was his brother and sister.

He loved his siblings, so he didn't see this as a job, but rather his responsibility to take care of his family. After all, his father was no longer there to be the man of the household. Determined to help his mother through this difficult time, Jeremiah never spoke of his father. He swallowed the spirit of curiosity and killed the need for closure by never asking why his father was no longer in his life. His greatest hero was now gradually diminishing into an urban legend. The guy who would run across the playground to lift him up into the air after arriving by the city transit system was slowly dwindling away like a figment of the imagination. Desperate to show his mother love and appreciation, Jeremiah found himself without a voice once again and dared not mention his father to his mother ever again. If only Catherine and Troy could understand what was truly going on.

Sometimes they would ask Gloria about their father, and if she was in a bad mood, she would respond with the wrath of Greek gods! Slash! Slash! Slash! Whipping from left to right, Gloria would strike the little ones with her belt as she yelled and screamed in a horrendous manner. Troy would take off running and screaming. Catherine would escape after taking several blows and proceeded to try her luck at hiding. "Bring your ass here too, because you're the oldest," said Gloria to Jeremiah as she extended her arm and pointed violently. Screams filled the air as the three children cried together and rubbed their wounds. "Keep crying and I'll really give yawl something to shed tears over!" Most of the pain Jeremiah experienced as a child was due to the fact he matured quickly on a mental basis, he understood his family was living in poverty, and he'd accepted an immense amount of responsibility at such a young age. It would be years before Troy or Catherine would come to realize how long Jeremiah had been making sacrifices in order to be the best role model he could possibly be.

Life, as unpredictable as it has proven to be, was about to take another unexpected turn. One day, Gloria returned home after a long day with a smile on her face. Go wash your hands and face, she would say repeatedly as she scrambled to change clothes. The three children made their way to the back and did as their mother instructed. Water splashed everywhere as the children played in the water. They were quite excited for leaving the mobile for once. The only break they could get from it was playing in the yard with their new favorite cousins.

A red truck pulled up outside in front of Lucille's house. "Let's go," said Gloria. Troy grabbed Catherine's hand, and Jeremiah helped them down the stairs of the trailer. Once on the ground, the two of them took off running and screaming and laughing hilariously down the paved driveway. The look on Gloria's face was of embarrassment, and Jeremiah wondered if the two would be disciplined in front of the stranger. "Stop running, you two," she said in a soft voice with a gentle smile on her face. Jeremiah looked from corner of his eye with a bombshell expression on his face.

This tall man with a scruffy beard and dark shades covering his eyes opened the driver door and proceeded to walk around toward us. His big black hand with a gold ring on his index finger reached toward Jeremiah to shake his hand. "This is my friend Marcus," said Gloria to her three kids. "Hi," the kids responded simultaneously. He reached over Troy's head to open the half door of his red pickup and leaned the passenger seat forward. "Let's go, guys," Marcus said to the kids as he held the door open. They all hopped in, and Marcus closed the doors after Gloria positioned herself elegantly in her seat. Jeremiah watched as Marcus gave a sensual look to his mother as he leaned his head down to allow his dark shades to slide down just enough to offer a glimpse of his eyes.

There was something about his eyes that sent chills down Jeremiah's spine. They accelerated down the road as rhythmic tunes danced from the speakers of the truck. Marcus and Gloria whispered and laughed in the front as Jeremiah watched Troy and Catherine play next to him in the backseat. "Wow," the kids said in harmony as they arrived at the gorgeous lake. With their eyes as big as baseballs, the children danced in their seats and watched with complete amazement as they cruised around the lake watching the boats sail across and jet skis zoom by them. The main road meandered around the entire lake, so the kids got to see everything along the way. Fish were jumping out of the water, birds were diving from the sky into the water, frogs were snatching bugs from flowers, kids were running and playing, older men were standing on the peer throwing their fishing rods, women were dancing and drinking beer, and smoke filled the air as BBQ grills were fired up around the pavilions along the lake.

Jeremiah had never witnessed such collective happiness from a bunch of strangers in one genuine setting. He gazed and exhaled deeply as he felt peace and serenity flow from the tip of his toes to the top of his head. Marcus pulled over into the parking spot next to a sandy playground and paved basketball court a hundred feet away from the lake. Everyone leapt from the truck in a frenzy. There the kids seemed to play for hours on the swing set and slide, basketball court, and in the grass as a never-ending game of freeze tag continued as the sun began to set and the fireflies filled the air. Marcus gathered everyone together and led them back to the truck, as it was finally time to leave that magical place. The kids continued to gander from the back seat of the pickup out the smaller side window as they drove off into the dark.

After a short nap, Jeremiah opened his eyes as he heard the engine cut off. "Where are we, mommy?" he asked his mother. With hands as warm as the morning sun in mid spring, she brushed his cheek and told him they had arrived at her friend Marcus's house. Jeremiah hesitated to get out of the truck as ferocious barking filled his body with anguish. He pulled his mother's dress as she comforted him and ensured everything would be alright as they walked up the wooden steps on the front porch of the light green house. Upon entering the front door, they were in the middle of the living room, and Marcus walked through to the kitchen. He returned with assorted crackers in his hand, and each of the children grabbed one. They scuffled onto the couch as Marcus placed a movie into the VHS player. Although Troy and Catherine were glued to the tv screen, Jeremiah noticed his mom and Marcus disappear down the dark hallway and into a bedroom before he heard a door close.

Not realizing how worn out he truly was, Jeremiah found himself dozing off in the stranger's home. The sun rose bright and early the next morning as the children yawned and stretched their arms and legs and wiggled their tiny fingers and toes. The smell of bacon overtook the house and Jeremiah slid from the couch with his curiosity spiked by the smell of breakfast cooking. He peeped around the white refrigerator which stood against the wall as you walked through the walkway into the kitchen. There his mother stood eight feet way cooking the best meal he ever had. As delightful as this was, Jeremiah was so confused. He couldn't figure out what was going. Yes, he was happy to be in a home with running water and electricity, but was this guy supposed to be his new dad?

His life continued to shift as things also changed back at home. Since their first visit with Marcus, Gloria spent a lot of time away. Either Jeremiah was given the responsibility to take care of the household in her absence, or Lucille was asked to step in. Although she agreed from time to time, her attitude quickly changed as her patience ran thin. Jeremiah even noticed brief arguments between his mom and aunt over the next couple of weeks. Lucille's treatment of the children changed drastically as meal portions were smaller, any act committed by the children in her house seemed to tick her off, and nasty looks were given often to the children. She even spoke badly of their mother while she was away as she grew tired of caring for more children without adequate compensation. Jeremiah would sit there as anger filled his pure heart, but he dared not speak back to his aunt because of the values instilled in him by his mother. Troy and Catherine would sit there sniffling as tears rolled down their blushed cheeks. As Lucille walked down the hall back to her room, Jeremiah leaned toward his siblings and said that everything was going to be okay. Shockingly, to some people, sharing the same bloodline meant little to nothing!

Chapter 3

A Turn for the Worse

Over the next couple of weeks, Lucille and Gloria were involved in many heated arguments. "What kind of parent are you to leave these kids here all the time while you're out running these streets?" Lucille asked Gloria.

"I don't know how you feel as though you have the authority to question me," Gloria responded. "I'm grown, honey, and I don't ask you to do a damn thing for me. I handle my own responsibilities and I don't need anyone to take care of me or my children. You always try to make yourself appear to be better than everyone else because you're supporting our sister's kids and go to church every week, but that doesn't make you a better person than me. We don't have to live here and take your bullshit! God will provide for me just as he provides for you. I may be down right now, honey, but this too shall pass!"

Gloria and Lucille shared a middle sister, Barber, who was physically handicapped and partially blind. She lived in a residential community across town for the elderly and handicapped, as she wasn't equipped to care for her own children. Gloria became infuriated with Lucille and her belittling comments, and she aggressively instructed her kids out of the house and back to the mobile home. Over the next couple of days, Jeremiah experienced horrid flashbacks as his mother woke up early each day and began stuffing bags with clothes.

The following week, one of Gloria's friends came to pick them up. Jeremiah and the others were excited as they thought it was finally time for another field trip with one of mommy's friends. Gloria pulled Jeremiah to the side. "Remember how much your mother loves you and cared for you, my sweet son. Be careful of what you say in here, because these people could rip us apart and we will never be together again. Stay strong, my dear boy; you got this!" Jeremiah remained in his seat consumed with anxiety, heart pumping fast, hands covered in perspiration as his nerves grew worse. The car turned and to the left appeared and tan brick building. The words were far too big for Jeremiah to pronounce, but three letters stood out: D-H-R.

As they walked into the building, there sat Lucille who'd obviously arrived much earlier. Gloria rolled her eyes and sat her children down across the room. A guy who seemed to be as old as Marcus but with a lighter skin complexion and smaller belly approached the family. "Hi, beautiful kids! I'm Mr. Krotcher, this is Ms. Sanders, and I'll be speaking with each of you today. Would you like a piece of candy?" The kids began eating the candy, and Jeremiah watched cautiously as Mr. Krotcher began speaking softly to Gloria. She took a quick glance at Jeremiah, and at that moment he now realized what his mother was referring too before they arrived. "Kids, follow me, and Mom, why don't you follow Ms. Sanders."

"I love y'all, be good," said Gloria with the sweetest smile on her face.

In the room with Mr. Krotcher were several toys, and Troy and Catherine didn't hesitate before sprinting off. "While the smaller ones play, I want to talk to you. Is that ok?" Jeremiah's heart pounded so fast and hard in his chest he thought Mr. Krotcher could both see and hear it! His fingers tapped his thigh nervously.

"Yes, that's fine!"

Mr. Krotcher began asking Jeremiah a series of questions. How is life at home? How do you feel about your mom? What role does your aunt play?

Do you like living with your mom? Would you rather live somewhere else? Do you guys eat well? Are there any conditions at home you don't like?

Jeremiah fought back the tears as the pressure placed on him to answer these questions in a manner which would not result in his family being ripped apart yet again was nearly insufferable. His mother had raised him to always tell the truth, but as he reflected on the talk he had with his mother earlier that morning, he felt the need to protect his family. He answered the questions the best way he knew how, saying things such as, "I love my mom and all she does for us. I love being around her and so does my brother and sister. We would never want to be separated from our mom because she loves us and does the best that she can!" Mr. Krotcher was blown away by such a mature response and smiled as he patted Jeremiah on the shoulder and said thank you. He asked Jeremiah if there was anything else he should know, and a quick "no" was given.

The kids were led into a different room where they saw their mother and aunt sitting across the table from one another. The three of them took off running and gave their mother a big hug, and she kissed each of them on the forehead. "Go over there and play," she said. Troy and Catherine played willingly while Jeremiah was too stressed to pretend to have fun. He listened as closely as he could as the adults talked more. "Based on the feedback of your son, we see no reason to place your children in a foster home. This is primarily due to your sister not being willing to take them in and the interview with your son Jeremiah. He delivered a compelling case on your behalf, and we would hate to separate this family. Some home inspections may be conducted to validate his statements, but as of now you're going to remain a family. Are there any other family members who may be able to help since Lucille is no longer willing?" A smirk grew across Gloria's face as the news was given to her, and Jeremiah smiled from across the room as he heard the good news.

"No," she replied. "I'm sure she's not interested since she found out the state wouldn't pay her for taking my kids in." Lucille looked ashamed and didn't respond.

A confused look swept across Jeremiah's face as his heart ached from hearing such harsh words. *My aunt doesn't want us if she can't get paid?* Jeremiah whispered this question to himself and dropped his head in disbelief. Mr. Krotcher and Ms. Sanders shook Gloria and Lucille's hand and waved goodbye to them. They ran over to their mother and proceeded to walk out the front door of the building. Gloria's friend was there waiting for them and they all hopped into the car, but not before Gloria gave Jeremiah the tightest hug he ever received from her, and she whispered, "I knew you could do it!" Jeremiah smiled but couldn't find the words to respond as he once again found himself in shock and speechless by the events that transpired just moments ago. This is too much, he thought to himself.

When they returned home, Gloria began grabbing the bags she started packing days ago, and before you knew it, Marcus pulled into the driveway and blew his horn. Jeremiah became a little frantic as he remembered being in this situation before, and he knew what to expect. "Come on, my babies, we're going with mommy's friend for a little while, so grab your things and let's go," said Gloria. Marcus helped grab a few things and placed them on the back of his pickup and once again they drove off to an unknown destination. It was dark last time they went to Marcus's house, so Jeremiah, despite his navigable skills, couldn't orientate himself.

When they arrived at Marcus's house, he guided them to the back room and showed them where to place their black trash bags full of clothes. "This is your new room," he said to them. There was one big bed, an old dresser with a mirror, and a closet. As the kids placed their things in the drawers, Marcus returned with more assorted crackers as a peace offering. They all smiled and continued to get organized in their new home. The trip to Marcus's house felt as though it took forever, and in the daylight Jeremiah could determine they moved even farther into the country. There were no streetlights along the roads and no stores within walking distance. All Jeremiah could see along both sides of the highway were houses, trees, a big church, and dogs chasing cats across the busy highway.

Things started off great, as their mother always prepared breakfast and dinner for the family. Life essentials they once lacked now flowed in abundance, from food, hot water, and electricity. There was even more time available for Jeremiah to be a kid once again. Days overflowed with laughter as the kids played various games in the fenced-in yard. One of their favorite games was playing house under the mimosa tree in the front yard. Jeremiah would pretend to be the dad while Troy and Catherine were the kids. He would make pretend dinner using leaves, dirt, water, and rocks to make food items such as pancakes, collard greens, corn, mashed potatoes, and even fried chicken. The kids played all summer long and enjoyed more trips to the lake with the magical adult juice in the cooler Marcus always stashed on the back of the truck. Troy and Catherine grew closer to Marcus, but Jeremiah held his reservations. He liked Marcus and thought he was a cool guy, but he wasn't his father!

All summer long, Marcus invited his friends over. When they arrived, the grill would be smoking as chicken wings, corn-on-the cob, smoked sausage, and baby back ribs simmered deliciously. There were always multiple tables with different guys. One table may feature a heated game of spades while the other had a wild game of dominoes. All the men had one thing in common—they loved the magic potion in the different colored containers. Jeremiah noticed how the potion made them all act differently. Their voices grew louder, language became foul, and dance moves were even more weird. Children weren't allowed around the grown folk, so Jeremiah glanced from afar as he saw his mother sit in Marcus's lap and laugh blissfully while staring into his eyes. Seeing her smile light up the night sky melted his heart. He immediately took off running to play with the others. Maybe everything would be alright after all!

Chapter 4

THE EVIL SPIRIT

The summer days grew shorter, and the natural nightlights twinkled in the sky earlier this time of year. Jeremiah never knew the stars shined so bright while living in the city with his dad. There were lights everywhere compared to living in the country where your porch light or flashlight were your only sources. Although Jeremiah had been living his best life playing with his siblings all summer long racing, climbing trees, chasing each other, tossing them into the air, playing at the playground by the lake, and playing hide and seek, red light-green light, and a host of other games, the time had finally come for his first day at the new school.

Jeremiah was stoked about meeting other kids his age. His mother ironed his clothes while he took a bath with his siblings. He was so excited that night that he jumped in bed immediately after his bath was over. Gloria tucked them in and wished them all a goodnight. Don't forget to say your prayers before going to sleep, she said to them before closing the bedroom door. The three children said together, "Now I lay me down to sleep. I pray the Lord my soul to keep. If I shall die before I wake, I pray to the Lord, my soul to take." Troy and Catherine snuggled under their big brother, and they all passed soundly asleep.

Ehhh! Ehhh! Ehhh! Ehhh! Sounded the alarm. Jeremiah sprung out of bed to turn off the alarm and ran rapidly to the bathroom to brush his teeth and wash his face. By the time his mom made it out of the room, he was already putting on his clothes. Gloria started greasing and brushing his hair. Jeremiah proceeded to put on his belt and tie his shoes. "Come here, boy," she said as she grabbed him by the arm and pulled him closer. She rubbed her hands together and then down his face, behind his ears, and around his neck. She smiled from ear to ear, looked him in the eyes, and said, "That's my bigga boy!" Jeremiah's heart lit up and became weightless as a feather. A warm sensation covered his entire body and he felt invincible as his mother walked him to the front door to wait for the bus. The front porch was only a five-second sprint away for Jeremiah to reach the end where the pavement from the porch connected to the edge of the road.

Jeremiah reached his new classroom and hesitated a moment before walking in completely. He glanced quickly around the room as his first-grade teacher, Mrs. Anderson, approached him. "Hi, you must be Jeremiah?"

"Yes, ma'am, he replied."

"Attention, class! This is our new student, Jeremiah." He began walking toward the nearest seat which was next to a dark-skinned boy with braids hanging down to his shoulders. As he sat down, the little boy said, "My name is Alex. Would you like to be my friend?"

"Sure, we can be friends," Jeremiah replied ecstatically.

He never missed a day of school after that day, the day he made his first best friend! His teacher loved him, and his classmates thought he was funny. He made many friends as they spent more time together during the morning session, on the playground during recess, and on the bus ride home. During the morning sessions, all the children hopped off the bus and gathered in the gymnasium before reporting to their first class. The school now was K-12, and it had a large gym with all the bleachers positioned on one side of the court. Banners and jerseys hung from the ceiling, and there was an office and bathrooms on the opposite side of the basketball court. Most of the kids gathered in smaller groups with their closest friends playing hand games, doing hair, joking around, and buying snacks from the concession stand. Most of the kids in the school knew each other because it was a small rural high school with only 450 students total. The morning times were the best to Jeremiah as he took chances to make friends, and he started by connecting with Alex.

He loved school and the one-on-one lessons with Mrs. Anderson writing his letters. He always blushed when she was around him. Jeremiah felt in his element as he made friends, learned new things in class, and shared crazy fun memories with his friends on the bus. When he reached home, the positive atmosphere would gradually descend. Gloria would greet him and ask about his day at school. Then Jeremiah had to go do chores, followed by his homework. There was no time to play until his business was handled, and then he could be with his siblings before eating dinner and going to bed.

Jeremiah loved the time his mom spent studying with him, but he sometimes believed she went overboard. One night, Jeremiah was in the tub taking a bath after doing his homework, and his mom suddenly entered the bathroom. He stood up instantly, holding his towel as his eyes noticed the belt in her hand. "What's your name?" she asked. He paused for a second, as if she was asking him a trick question.

"Jeremiah," he replied in a frightened tone.

"Spell it," she commanded. As Jeremiah attempted to spell his name and failed miserably the first couple times, Gloria struck Jeremiah for every letter he got wrong. Minutes passed before Jeremiah finally spelled his name correctly as he cried and rubbed his legs and butt.

"Your name is Jeremiah; never forget who you are, my son." She helped her son get out of the bathtub and let him get dressed for bed.

The next few weeks went by and Jeremiah continued to progress at school and enjoyed the weekends at home with his siblings. However, he noticed his mom was spending an awful amount of time with the neighbors next door. Their house seemed old, dark, and mysterious. You never saw kids there, but a random old Chevrolet would be parked in the front yard.

A woman lived there, and she was short like Jeremiah's mom, but with a deep raspy voice. Jeremiah could hear her voice from time to time as she laughed and joked with Gloria as she returned home from her visits. Jeremiah could always sense the evil spirit that lingered around his mom whenever she returned from the house next door.

November finally came, and joy filled the house as Jeremiah's birthday was vastly approaching. He worried about the weather and if it would continue to be pleasant or if the conditions would change. Jeremiah rose from his bed early on his birthday. He walked over to the window in the room he shared with his siblings and opened the blinds. It was a cloudy, overcast day, and thick fog waiting to greet him on his seventh birthday. Sadness invaded his body as the look upon his face drooped into a frown. Unfortunately for Jeremiah, the rest of the day followed the gloomy start. There were no cake or candles waiting for him that day, nor any ice scream to slurp on. Later that evening, when he thought it was all over, Jeremiah received a gift from his mom. Jeremiah abruptly unwrapped the gift in the middle of the living room as he discovered a remote-controlled monster truck=. "Oh, yeahhh!" he shouted. They all laughed, and Jeremiah played with his truck until it was time for bed.

On the weekends, Gloria would wake the kids up early in the morning to get dressed. Marcus worked periodically on the weekends, and sometimes his mom kept the truck for the day. After so much time together, Troy and Catherine built a special bond with Marcus, but Jeremiah never opened up completely. There was a wall built between them, and Jeremiah didn't know how to break it down, or if he wanted it down.

During one of the Saturday drop-offs, Troy and Catherine gave Marcus a big hug and said, "I love you, Daddy." Jeremiah's heart pounded against his chest as he heard those words. He sat there confused and didn't know if he was supposed to say it too. He watched as Marcus's face was highlighted by a big smile and he reached down to hug them. Gloria had a heartwarming smile on her face as well. Seeing the connection between the three of them, Jeremiah fought to say the words too, but all he could muster was an empty hug to share with Marcus. As Marcus walked away from the truck waving goodbye, Jeremiah turned to the window in a last desperate attempt to pull his lips apart and speak the words, but nothing came from his mouth.

During the ride home, Jeremiah sat there feeling broken and puzzled. *What's wrong with me? Is something wrong with me? Why couldn't I speak? Am I supposed to call him Dad?* These were a few of the thoughts wondering through his young mind. Jeremiah was determined to be a part of the family, so when the next opportunity came, he did it. Just like any other Saturday morning, Marcus walked around the truck as Gloria exchanged seats. Troy and Catherine had already said I love you and given him a hug. Jeremiah walked him around the truck and onto the sidewalk in front of his building. His body temperature rose as his heart pounded faster and faster and faster. Jeremiah leaned his head out the window as Marcus began walking away, and he yelled, "Bye, dad!" Marcus turned back around and waved goodbye with a smile on his face. Jeremiah waved back and returned to his seat with a vibrant smile on his face as well. *Yes, I did it!* he thought to himself. *Things can definitely change now.*

Many weeks passed. Fall turned into winter and winter into early spring. Jeremiah had been noticing heated arguments between his mother and Marcus. Gloria was standing in the kitchen after Marcus left the house. "Oh, baby, I know how to get you. If you think I'm going to stand in this kitchen and cook all these meals for you, you got another thing coming. Watch this!" Gloria said to herself as she stormed to the back room. Jeremiah noticed his mom was getting dressed. As she combed her hair, she danced in the mirror, snapping her fingers.

"Are you ok, ma?" Jeremiah asked in a timid voice.

"Oh yes, baby! Mama has everything under control. One monkey doesn't stop a show around here. Mama always has a backup plan." She turned back around with a smile on her face and continued to put on makeup. Jeremiah watched his mom dance a little longer before walking away. He had no idea what his mother meant by a backup plan, but he would soon find out.

The next weekend, Marcus left earlier that day with his cooler and the magic potion. Gloria was in her room getting dressed when the doorbell rang. Gloria rushed to the door in her gripping purple dress with a low v-cut, and there stood Lucille in a blue dress with white pearls stitched on the shoulder and a tall dark-skinned lady in a tight black dress with a split coming up her left thigh. The ladies were surely about to have a great time. They all hugged and laughed in high-pitched voices, and the kids all laughed, as they'd never seen them like this before. Gloria leaned down to Jeremiah. "You know my rules. Don't open my door, don't answer my phone, and don't let your brother and sister tear up my house!" Jeremiah nodded his head in agreement.

The ladies returned later that night to drop off Gloria. Marcus beat them home and had already made it to bed. Jeremiah ran to open the door, and he noticed the lady in the black dress falling as she tried to help his mom who was also falling. He jumped down to help, and after several attempts, they finally made it up the back stairs and through the kitchen door. Lucille and the other lady left after they made it into the house. "Go to bed, baby; everything is ok," she said to Jeremiah. As he turned around and took a step, he saw Marcus coming down the hall. Marcus didn't even look his way as he walked angrily toward Gloria. Jeremiah continued to walk but kept his eye on his mom. The two adults began to argue, and Jeremiah covered his ears as his brother and sister woke up from hearing the ruckus and started crying. After standing there in the hallway and closing his eyes, Jeremiah ran into the room to comfort Troy and Catherine. "It's ok! Shhh! It's ok! Shhh!" He repeated over and over until he was able to stop them from crying.

Minutes, although it felt like a lifetime, passed, and everything went silent. Moments later, they heard footsteps down walking up the hall, and in through the door walked their mom. She stumbled slightly but made a safe landing on the bed where she kissed each of her children.

"Go to bed, babies. Mama's ok. Go to sleep." She walked out the door and closed it behind her. Jeremiah could hear as their bedroom door closed moments later. He listened closely as two separate pairs of footsteps walked through the room. He heard the sound of them sitting on the mattress, and seconds later—THUMP! Jeremiah heard the tumultuous thump on the floor and a scratching sound against the wall. Jeremiah and his siblings all cried softly together as they thought their mom had been physically kicked out of bed. Back and forth Jeremiah rocked his siblings as he held them closely while tears rolled down his face. This time, he couldn't find the words to say it was going to be alright. He couldn't say anything at all, as he was once again voiceless.

Chapter 5

BEYOND BROKEN

Jeremiah just couldn't get past the recent events of his life and how the battles seemed to never end. Things were so intense, the family didn't celebrate Troy or Catherine's birthday either, aside from eating a cake. His mother always told him he had to be strong, but he often wondered, *Why us?* He sat there on the edge of the bed and closed his eyes as impactful thoughts of his mother flooded his brain. He reflected back to the time his mother called him to her room.

"Jeremiah, do you know where your name came from?"

Jeremiah stood there like a deer caught in headlights and shook his head no.

"Your name came from the Bible, and it's a powerful name, my son, with an immense amount of responsibility. Never forget that! Do you know where in the Bible your name is located?"

Jeremiah shook his head again, no.

Gloria handed her son a Bible for the first time and watched as her son searched anxiously through it to find his name. Jeremiah couldn't fully read at the time, but as he flipped through the pages, he found it. His head lifted in slow motion as he now realized why his mother went to the extreme of teaching him how to spell his name and where it came from. Page after page he saw his name, and suddenly he jumped into his mother's arms as he glowed with promise.

    Marcus's attitude changed over the next couple of days as his birthday was drawing near. His birthday was only five days after Jeremiah's, and this year he was throwing a joint party. Finally, the big day arrived and music blasted loudly from the speakers in the living room windows facing outside. Several of Marcus's friends showed up with coolers ready to celebrate, and many of Jeremiah's relatives showed up as well. Lucille came with April, Rebecca, and Jonathan. One of Jeremiah's oldest sisters he hadn't seen in years even came with her older boyfriend. The neighbor next door dropped by unexpectedly on Jeremiah's account. He'd never seen her up close, so he peaked around the small magnolia sampling in the yard to get a better look without being seen.

    The adults laughed and danced as the kids laughed and played their little hearts out. Jeremiah walked around all night and collected money from the adults. Gloria bragged to everyone about how smart he was, and Jeremiah blushed in embarrassment. As the sunlight dimmed and the colors changed, people began to leave, one car at a time, with to-go plates stacked to the ceiling. The remaining adults grabbed their final drinking potions and walked home. Jeremiah saw his mother and the neighbor whispering as he entered the house. *My mom is always different when she hangs around her,* Jeremiah thought to himself. Such a curious mind he had, and hopefully he'd find out the truth soon. As Jeremiah sat on his bedroom floor, he counted his collected earnings. $25! $26! $27! Jeremiah felt like a rich man holding all his money.

    The bedroom door creeped open and his mom walked in. He noticed something different in her eyes tonight. She was beside herself, and something else had taken over as she looked at him with widened eyes. "Hey, my baby! You want to be mamma's bigga boy?" she asked politely. There it was again, his favorite nickname that only his mother called him. Only this time, it didn't make him feel warm and fuzzy. It felt like a trick. It felt untrue! "Let momma borrow your birthday money, and I'll give it back to you." She reached down to grab the money and Jeremiah said ok and let it go. Tears formed in his eyes as she kissed him on the forehead, but they didn't fall until she turned around and walked out the door. His head dropped to his knees as the door closed and tears hit like lava as they dropped from his chin. Flashes of all the suspicious acts committed by his mother appeared in his head as he wondered why she needed the money. For the first time, he didn't trust his mother's words, as he saw the dark spirit take over through her widened and glossy eyes. Jeremiah squeezed his eyes tightly and cringed his teeth together in an effort to stop the thoughts, because he didn't want to know the truth. He slept there in the fetal position until the next morning.

Weeks later, nothing seemed to change in the house as things remained hostile. Jeremiah ended the school year with all A's, and not even his big achievement could turn the sour situation. All the extra studying with his mother actually paid off, and all he wanted to do was celebrate, but unfortunately, his big moment had the wrong timing. As the summer started, Marcus's appetite for the potion increased as he spent more time hanging out and less time working. Some days Gloria was in a good mood, and others she spiraled downward as she spent more time next door. Marcus returned home reeking of his afternoon drinks and stared at the kids as he walked through the door. He tripped over a toy lying on the floor but caught his footing preventing the fall. "What did I tell y'all about leaving toys all over the house?" he asked as he reached for the snake skin belt hanging on the wall leading to the hallway. He grabbed Jeremiah by the arm with one hand and held him in the air while whipping him forcefully with the belt in the other hand. His scream echoed throughout the house, and his petrified siblings cried on the couch, as Marcus had struck them too.

As the sun dropped, a beautiful full moon danced across the sky while stars shined brighter than ever. Jeremiah looked upon the night sky and wondered about his life. "Why hasn't my dad saved us? Where is he? I knew better than to trust Marcus. I can't believe I called him Dad!" he thought to himself with his chin dropping to his chest while Troy and Catherine slept peacefully in bed. Jeremiah jumped as he heard a frantic shout come from the living room. He crept from the bed and opened the door slowly as lots of rumbling came from the front of the house. Tip-toeing down the hall in the darkness, he suddenly saw his mom holding a gun and pointing it at drunken Marcus. "Don't move, asshole! I'm tired of your shit!" Gloria shouted in a hoarse voice while squeezing the handle of the gun tighter. Soft cries grew louder and filled with terror as Troy and Catherine walked out of the room and saw Gloria holding the gun.

"Mommy, don't," they screamed! Gloria started crying harder than before, and Marcus reached down slowly and grabbed the three children.

Marcus asked, "Is that what you want to do, to shoot me in front of your kids?" He pulled the kids closer to him as they all reached out for their mother, crying. The staredown between him and Gloria seemed to last a lifetime. Jeremiah could smell the potion leaking from Marcus's pores, and as he glanced at his mother, he saw the same widened eyes controlled by another. "Put down the gun," Marcus shouted! Gloria instructed him to let her kids go, and he did so, but cautiously. Gloria lowered the gun slowly as tears dropped and mixed with the blood on the floors.

Gloria hugged her kids as Marcus grabbed the gun while running to the back of the house cursing ungodly. While Gloria comforted her weeping kids, Marcus returned to the front with two black trash bags full of clothes. "Get your shit and get out," he said to Gloria and her kids.

"I can't believe you're going to kick us out in the middle of the night! What kind of man are you? You know I don't have a car!" Gloria said desperately. Marcus replied with an impetuous, "Get out!"

Gloria picked up little Catherine, wrapped her legs around her waist, and grabbed Troy by the hand. Jeremiah took after his mother and grabbed the two garbage bags with clothes. They walked out the door and embarked on their journey down the indistinct country road without a phone or dime to their name. They'd only made it a half mile before they heard the rumbling in the sky, soon followed by streaks of flashing lights. Small raindrops commenced to fall on the poor family as they walked the lonely street. Troy and Catherine started crying because they were afraid of storms. Jeremiah began to struggle as the bags felt heavier and heavier the longer they walked. Jeremiah felt broken as his arms and fingers grew numb from carrying the bags. "Please help me, Lord," prayed Gloria as she adjusted the kids in her arms. Living fifteen miles from town never seemed so long, and Jeremiah thought it would never end.

Suddenly, a dark sedan passed slowly by them. They all watched the car and hoped for a sign. There is was! The red brake lights on the car lit up, followed by the white reverse lights. They all ran to the stranger's car, and Gloria asked for a ride. The bearded old man told them to hop in, and they did without hesitation. The old man asked Gloria lots of questions about what happened, and she provided the stranger with details as he drove them safely down the road. Jeremiah heard his mother ask the man to take her to Lucille's house as he started to drift into his own thoughts. Chills crawled up Jeremiah's spine as he pictured his mom holding that gun with her finger on the trigger, pointing it at Marcus. *Is this all a dream?* Once again he was completely blown away by his life, and how they went through constant pain that never seemed to end.

Finally, they arrived at Lucille's house. Gloria thanked the old man over and over as she opened her door. She walked around and opened the back door to help Jeremiah with Troy and Catherine. Gloria carried Troy because he was bigger, and Jeremiah carried dainty Catherine to the front door. They rang the doorbell multiple times before Lucille finally opened the door. April and Rebecca were sleep, but Jonathan was peeping from his room door. Gloria took Catherine to the girls' room, and the boys went into the room with their cousin Jonathan.

It had been forever since Jeremiah saw his cousin, and he had grown so tall. "Would y'all like some pancakes?" Jonathan asked them. Troy and Jeremiah looked at each other with big smiles on their faces, and they replied yes. Jonathan left and returned to the room after thirty minutes with two plates in his hand. He handed one to Troy and the other to Jeremiah. He played his guitar while the two boys ate the delicious pancakes topped with butter and swimming in syrup. Jeremiah finished first, but Troy followed soon after. Jonathan grabbed the plates and took them to the kitchen. When he returned, he saw how Jeremiah grew fixated on his guitar and offered him to play. Jeremiah reached for the guitar excitedly, and Jonathan showed him how to hold it. Jeremiah looked over to Troy, but he was already sound asleep. It didn't take long before Jeremiah was fast asleep behind his little brother after such a formidable day for an eight-year-old.

The next morning, Lucille had Rebecca and April in the kitchen with her cooking breakfast. Jeremiah and the others rushed to the bathroom to freshen up. They all circled around the kitchen table as Aunt Lucille placed the prepared plates in front of each child. Each of them bowed their heads and said grace before digging into the plates. As good as the food was, Aunt Lucille was particular about portion control. Every meal felt like a tease, as she only cooked just enough for everyone to sample. After two glasses of ice water, it would always fill the belly, though.

Gloria left earlier that morning before the children woke up. Lucille told her she had three days to find out what she was going to do, and then she had to go. Gloria returned late on the third day in a green coupe driven by a dark-skinned man with ear loops and a thin mustache. He couldn't have been more than six feet tall. Gloria stood from the passenger seat, closed the door, and the car drove off while the man waved. Gloria walked up the driveway with a different sway in her hips, confidence glowing from her face.

The same car returned the next morning, and Gloria gathered their things and instructed her kids to go to the car. She kissed Lucille on the cheek and closed the door behind her. The man walked around from the driver's door and reached for the bags. "This is momma's friend, Patrick." He shook each of their hands before placing the bags in the trunk. Jeremiah squinted his eyes to look through the man's glasses, but they were too dark to see his eyes. Troy sat behind Patrick, Catherine in the middle, and Jeremiah behind his mother. Zooming down the highway heading south with the windows down and wind blowing freely, Jeremiah closed his eyes and took a deep, liberating breath.

Chapter 6

NEVER LOSE FAITH

The sun rose and set dozens of times as the poor family managed to restart their lives after such a tragic turn. Life never seemed to give Gloria and her kids too long of a break from chaos. When would the horror stories end for the Walker family? Was the family cursed? Would Jeremiah and his siblings ever experience a normal childhood? Was normal overrated?

One glorious Saturday morning, Jeremiah and his siblings woke up as their mother and Patrick were in the kitchen of the small single-wide mobile home making breakfast. The trailer was small, but at least this time they had running water and electricity again, so everything seemed better than the way it used to be. The scent that occupied the air was from something they'd never had before. Jeremiah walked into the kitchen and noticed square pieces of meat frying in the pan. "What's this?" he asked as he stood there pointing at the pan.

"It's deer sausage," replied Patrick. Patrick was a true man of the country, as he enjoyed hunting and fresh deer meat. He could eat it year-round if it was available. He loved to walk around barefooted through the yard as the kids played, and he often tried to play with them, as he was still a kid at heart. He purchased a football to play catch with the boys in the yard and frequently spoiled Catherine with any snack she wanted from the store. Patrick didn't have much, and he lived a simple life. There was one thing that stood out about Patrick compared to the other men Gloria shared in the life, and it was that Patrick never lived in one place too long. Jeremiah never understand why, but he did his best to accept the new adventurous lifestyle without suspicion. He just wanted everything to work out for once.

This first place they lived was in a small, mixed town, but predominantly white. Jeremiah's school was mixed, and he noticed many faces and features he'd never seen before. From red hair, freckles, and blonde eyelashes which looked invisible, to Mohawks! At Jeremiah's previous school, he excelled academically and remained in the top three percent of his class. Here at the new school, things were different. Jeremiah switched from multiple classes throughout the day, and the teachers often gifted free recess to well-behaved students. Jeremiah received multiple recess passes, but he never knew what to do. He walked the halls and ventured to the open play space hoping to find other kids to monitor how they behaved and wondered if he could make any new friends.

A few weeks passed and Jeremiah seemed to adjust well in his new environment. Back at home, things were going smoothly, as far as he could tell. Once again, the children lived in an area where there were no other kids to play with, so life continued for Troy and Catherine as it always had. Troy was getting older and finally approaching the age to attend kindergarten. Their days were spent playing in the yard and next door with the neighbor's dog. The neighbors lived in a fairly big, two-story blue home with a large, white, house dog that loved Catherine. From time to time the neighbors would be visited by their children and grandkids. This provided an awesome opportunity for the kids to make new friends. Anytime Jeremiah, Troy, and Catherine went over, the neighbors gave them yogurt. Jeremiah was never a fan of yogurt, so he only ate a little in front of the neighbors and gave the rest to Troy when they returned to the house.

Patrick seemed to treat Gloria well, and they enjoyed each other's company. Jeremiah watched how they interacted with one another and how much his mother laughed and smiled genuinely compared to their life with Marcus. *Is this the plan B my mother spoke of?* Jeremiah asked himself as he sat on the couch. Jeremiah didn't know much of anything about this guy, and his mom never gave background stories of the guys she dated after his father. Other than the few memories he held onto about his father, Jeremiah realized he didn't know much at all about him either. All this time they were spending apart wasn't helping the situation, either. Time never seemed to stop, and nothing brought him closer to his father.

As Jeremiah grew accustomed to the new school and remote neighborhood over the next few weeks, Patrick began transporting the family to their new location. This new town seemed to be similar in many ways from the level of diversity to the remoteness of their home. However, the living conditions were worse. Once again, they were living in a home without running water, but this time there was electricity. The family shared one heater, so Gloria went back to old tactics and sectioned off the house to help fight the winter cold. Jeremiah had to learn the process of fetching water from the well outside next to the house. Every day he would gather water from the well and his mother would boil it on the stove, filter it through a cloth to catch sediment and bugs and into a different pale, and then she placed it in the fridge to cool before allowing the kids to drink it.

Most baths were taken either in the sink or in the tub after fetching buckets of water from the well. An iron conductor of some sort was used to heat the water over a period of time before everyone would take a bath. You had to plug into the wall before the iron would turn as hot as fire. It took forever for the water to become tolerable, but this was their new way of life, so they did their best to adjust without complaining. On the weekends, Gloria gathered the dirty clothes to her washing station which included a circular tin pan and a washboard. One clothing article at a time, Gloria scrubbed and pressed them against the washboard. When she grew tired, Jeremiah asked to help her, and she would stand to the side and smoke her cigarettes. Jeremiah never liked seeing his mother smoke, but she did it for years, and it seemed to be her habit.

Life was hard for the Walker family during the early and late 90s, and the kids were forced to learn tough lessons at an early age. For the past two years around each of their birthdays and Christmas, the kids had to hear the harsh truth. "Your birthday and Christmas are just another day! Be happy you're alive and give God praise for blessing you with life. Nobody ever gave me anything in life, and I don't have anything to give you!" These are the words Jeremiah took to heart as he grew depressed every year he or his siblings didn't receive anything. Again, Troy and Catherine were too young at this point to fully grasp the meaning of those words. Each year they would still approach their mom and make requests. Jeremiah would listen with sadness in his heart, as he knew they would be disappointed.

Christmas was approaching, and each day it got closer Jeremiah watched and listened as his mother cried. A confused look rested on Jeremiah's face as she cried. *I thought she said Christmas is just another day so don't ask for anything. Why is mother crying?* Jeremiah would say to himself. Jeremiah finally realized the hurtful words expressed by his mother weren't because she was cold-hearted, but because she loved them so much she didn't want them to be disappointed in her. Gloria didn't want her kids to view her as a failure or an incompetent mother. After watching his mother break down, Jeremiah ran to the back of the house to the room he shared with his siblings and reached in the closet. He pulled out a shoebox from under the clutter. Jeremiah had recently discovered his talent for saving money after the tragic moment of his birthday, and he hid every penny he could find. "Here, mom, I have some money so you can buy something." Jeremiah handed Gloria the shoebox with pennies, nickels, dimes, quarters, and a few dollar bills. Gloria sobbed even harder as she realized her son had the purest heart of gold. She reached out and pulled him close for a hug. "I love you, my son," she said. "Take your money and put it back," she instructed.

Everyone woke up early Christmas morning. Gloria walked into the kid's bedroom with swollen, puffy eyes, as she'd been crying all night from the thoughts of her children spending another lonely and empty holiday together. Suddenly, the doorbell rang. Everyone stared with a shocked look on their faces because they weren't expecting any company. Gloria opened the front door as she wiped tears from her face, and there stood one of her older daughters, Nicole. Gloria had seven kids all together, but the older children moved out to stay with other relatives or friends of the family years ago. Nicole hadn't been around to visit the family since before the family left the city to live with Lucille. *Where has she been all this time?* Jeremiah thought to himself. Gloria and Nicole hugged for what seemed like forever as they cried in each other arms.

"I got something for y'all," she said as she kneeled down to comfort her younger siblings. Nicole ran to the car where her boyfriend stood and opened the truck of their car. One, two, three, four, and even more boxes Nicole pulled from the trunk of the car!

"Presents!" All the kids shouted as they ran full speed to the car.

Gloria started crying all over again, but for the first time in years she was crying tears of joy. The children helped Nicole bring the gifts in the house as everyone grabbed what their names were on. "I've been searching for y'all so long," Nicole said as tears fell from her face. "I didn't know what happened to y'all or where you've been, but I kept praying for the Lord to direct me! I'm so happy I never gave up!" Nicole looked around and evaluated how they'd been living, and she shook her head. "Momma, I can't let y'all stay here like this. You have to come home with me." Gloria nodded her head in agreement as she cried even more from her daughter's generosity. All Gloria seemed to want was a little help. After spending a moment playing and laughing at each other, Nicole instructed the kids to pack what they could and put their things in the car. Nicole's boyfriend Jeremy helped the kids organize their belongings in the truck space. Gloria kissed her boyfriend goodbye and followed her kids outside to the car. As the car pulled off, Jeremiah looked back for one last glance, hoping this would be the last time his family would have to move or live in such conditions.

Chapter 7

Setting the Stage

After a few months of living with Nicole, Gloria ended up renting her own place. Things didn't quite work out as they all hoped. Nicole was a beautiful young lady with her hair cut into a bob, and her bangs hung over one eye, giving her a mischievous appearance. She had a wonderful sense of humor just like her mother, and loved being the center of attention. Nicole was a guardian angel in the eyes of her younger siblings by swooping in and saving them from the nightmare they were forced to live. Jeremiah reminisced on how Nicole glowed as she stood in the doorway after Gloria opened it on the Christmas morning. The light from the morning sun was so bright that you couldn't see her face as she stood there. All you could see was this human figure standing as bright white lights propelled from the figure. You couldn't see who she was until she stepped past the doorway and entered the house. It appeared as if an angel had stepped down from heaven.

Nicole's intentions were true when she gathered her family from the disturbing lifestyle, but just because you want something to work doesn't mean that's what's meant to happen. Nicole and Gloria's personalities were so similar, and that didn't prove to be a good thing. Additionally, Nicole had a short fuse in this stage of her life from unresolved issues in her past that she never spoke of before.

There was a significant age difference between Gloria's kids. They age gap between Nicole and Jeremiah gave the impression that Gloria had two batches of kids. As the first batch got older and moved out, Troy and Catherine were babies, and Jeremiah was considerably small as well.

Strangely, each of the older kids moved out to live on their own around the ages of fifteen and sixteen. It would be a few years before Jeremiah realized the lifestyle he was living didn't start with him. For one reason or another, Nicole, Thomas, Olivia, and Orlando all moved out. Orlando moved out to live with his high school track coach. After graduating, he left with a group of friends to travel the world and wouldn't be seen for years to come.

Olivia wasn't fortunate enough to graduate high school after moving out. She ended up falling in love with a dear friend, and they moved into an apartment to prepare for their first child two years after leaving home. Thomas didn't finish high school either due to bad behavior and frequent fighting. Jeremiah wondered what ever happened to him, but he soon learned Thomas was arrested and put in jail. Thomas was simply at the wrong place at the wrong time, and with the wrong cousin. He was spending years behind bars because a cousin on his father's side turned on him after robbing a store and blamed it all on Thomas. Meanwhile, the cousin was released based on his testimony because Thomas didn't talk. Unfortunately for Thomas, not everyone lives by the street code.

On the morning Gloria packed to leave the city, Nicole was the only older child living in the house. She was spending a few nights at her best friend's house. When she returned home to the apartment, she saw that clothes had been packed and her family had fled without her. She stood there in the empty apartment feeling completely alone. Jeremiah didn't know if she ran away and decided to move out, and all Nicole knew for sure was that she felt utterly alone. She cried and went back to live with her friends before falling in love with Jeremy. They lived in a single-wide trailer next door to Jeremy's aunt. They'd been renting the trailer for quite some time, and Jeremiah was amazed at all Nicole had accomplished as a teenager. Nicole even went back to get her GED because she didn't want to feel like a failure or quitter. She was doing well for herself.

With the unresolved resentment toward her mother and the new stress of trying to provide for her mother and younger siblings, it was simply too much to handle for such a broken spirit. Gloria didn't contribute to the matter because she didn't work at the time, so she couldn't pitch in financially to help around the house. Due to their previous lifestyle, a financial crisis was the quickest way to invoke stress and negative energy into the family's living space. Nicole wasn't the best at dealing with conflict. She was the same as Thomas with the bad temperament. She used to fight all the time at their old home. It wasn't too far from where she currently lived, because she remained in the city but lived on the east side now. She fought all the time in their old neighborhood. She often made Jeremiah fight to be sure he was tough and could handle himself.

Honestly, she loved seeing her brother fight because he always won, and when living in the projects, victories in battle matter. Jeremiah recalled the time four boys tried to jump him while walking home from school. He ran to tell his sister what happened and she immediately leapt from her seat on the steps of their apartment building. "Show them to me," she said to her brother. Nicole removed her belt as Jeremiah pointed out the first boy. Nicole and her homegirl took off running to catch him. As they grabbed the boy by the playground, Nicole handed the belt to Jeremiah. "Here, whoop him," she said with a grin on her face. "This will teach them to fight one-on-one next time." Jeremiah took the belt and struck the boy several times. One by one, they chased the bullies down and served them a nice southern ass whooping just like their mother gave them. Jeremiah, Nicole, and her friend all laughed as they returned to their apartment building on the other side of the basketball court that was erected between the playground and another apartment building. Jeremiah looked up to his sister since that moment. He wondered if she still fought like she used to as he daydreamed about the past.

One day, Nicole came to visit her mom in their new home. Things were going well for once. Gloria was maintaining a steady job, paying the bills, and her normal complexion had even returned to its natural radiant golden shine. Nicole was impressed and happy to see she let the evil go, even if it was temporary. Although things didn't work out with them living with her, she missed Troy and the others. "Y'all should come visit me for a few days," she said. Jeremiah, Troy, and Catherine packed their bags for the weekend and sprinted to the car. On their way to her trailer, Nicole and Jeremy stopped at Payless to buy shoes for the kids. She saw the ones they were wearing and how worn out they were. Next, they stopped by Walmart to get ingredients for dinner. Nicole loved making sloppy joe sandwiches. It became their tradition every time they came to visit her for the weekend.

Jeremiah had a hard time trying to figure out what Jeremy did exactly for work. He always had money, but he "worked" funny hours for a job. During one of their visits, Jeremiah asked if he could ride with Jeremy. Jeremy was tall, dark skinned, and had short dreads he often wore back into a ponytail. He had two gold teeth on the opposite sides of his mouth at the top. Jeremy liked to play his music loud, and Jeremiah loved it. They drove around the suburban neighborhoods, and Jeremy would meet different people. They'd shake hands for a few seconds and chat for a minute or so before driving off. Later they would travel to a house that sat off the road maybe seventy-five feet and surrounded by shrubs. From the outside, it looked abandoned, and Jeremiah wondered why he would hang out in such a place carrying a backpack. As they drove around, Jeremiah mimicked Jeremy as he nodded and grooved to the vibes of the music. Jeremy suddenly reached to turn down the music. "You know I love your sister and would do anything for that girl. She has my heart, and that's real!" He dapped Jeremiah as they both smiled and drove back home.

Jeremiah loved visiting his sister and her boyfriend. Sunday approached more quickly than desired, and the kids prepared to go back home in the country. They hated living so far away from their sister now that they'd reconnected. It was only a forty-five-minute drive from the city to where they lived, but it felt like forever away since Jeremiah's mother didn't have a car. When they arrived at the house, Gloria was sitting on the porch of the white house with black trim as if she knew they were on the way. Jeremiah and his siblings launched up the steps to take their belongings inside. Jeremiah noticed that after every trip his mother and Jeremy talked for an awfully long time before shaking hands and driving off. Jeremiah had noticed this handshake before as he peeked through the vanilla blinds.

Jeremiah, Troy, and Catherine returned to the doorway to wave goodbye to their sister as she drove off. Over the next few weeks, they made friends with two kids that lived next door. They finally lived near kids their age and could make friends. They played kickball together, picked plums from the trees, and walked the dirt roads by their house while throwing rocks at squirrels. On Sundays, Gloria made sure the kids were dressed and ready for the church bus. During the week, each of the kids rode the bus to school.

As the seasons changed, conditions around the house began backsliding to the old ways. The first thing to go was the cable; the kids never had it before but quickly figured out what they'd been missing. Next, the house phone was cut off, followed by the hot water. They were back to heating water on the stove to mix with the cold water in the tub to take a bath. It was a process, but the family made due until they were eventually able to have the services reconnected.

Patrick started reappearing, but this time in a different car. Jeremiah noticed how they spent a lot of time in the back room of the house. He would seldom walk over to sneak a peek. He could never see anything, and he only heard mumbling. He could never make out the words of their conversation. There was always one common denominator; a weird, burning smell.

Things weren't any better at school for Jeremiah. Since they moved, he now had to attend the big middle school in the city limits instead of the smaller high school in the country. The Board of Education decided to close his old school because it shrunk in size despite the school having the highest test scores in the county. The kids were at a different pace than what Jeremiah was used to. All the kids seemed to be consumed by sex, gangs, and sports. Jeremiah was often bullied because he was obviously poorer than his classmates. They made fun of his shoes and hand-me-down uniforms. Jeremiah felt trapped as he battled becoming another violent and angry child living in a single-parent home. He felt the pressure every day as the bullying seemed to never end. He tried everything he could to stop the name calling. Week after week they picked on him with poor jokes. Jeremiah tried to let his personality win them over. It was obvious he would never be in the popular crowd, but he only wanted the harassment to stop.

He witnessed as all his friends who also attended the smaller school were converted to gang members, disruptive students, pregnant, and obsessed with sex. Down to earth, intelligent, and athletic kids were all lost in the city-limit school district. Jeremiah felt conflicted because he had made his mother a promise to stay away from such temptation. Gloria, fearful of her last three children turning out like her oldest kids, made Jeremiah promise to stay away from sexual temptation. She gave him a long speech from time to time about how they didn't graduate from high school and achieve their life goals. He could still remember the hurt in his mother's voice as she delivered her speech. Meanwhile, he was faced daily with guys who attempted to provoke him into a fight and picked on him for being a virgin. *Will it ever end?* he would ask silently in his prayers.

Chapter 8

TRIAL AND ERROR

School used to be Jeremiah's center of liberation. He couldn't control his life or how they lived. Jeremiah couldn't control the demons in his life either. However, there was one thing he was good at—making good grades. Jeremiah may not have been the best dressed or come from the wealthiest background, but he could outperform any student. From straight A's, Student of the Month, 100 Outstanding Students in the State, and consecutive semesters on the honor roll, Jeremiah was quite the decorated scholar. Due to his financial restrictions, he wasn't able to pay membership fees for clubs or attend the many field trips. However, ending the school year with the highest grade in his courses meant the world to him. His grade point average was the only thing he seemed to have influence over, and most times his grades and academic success were the only positivity in his life to keep him on the straight and narrow.

Back at home, Patrick continued to visit more and more. It was a coincidence that every time he reappeared in their lives, Gloria would change in both her actions and appearance. It was hard to notice at first, but soon Jeremiah noticed it all, even the demon that caused her eyes to widen, accompanied by constricted pupils and weight loss. One night, Patrick was over and Jeremiah noticed scars all over his legs. As he looked closer, the marks were all over his arms as well.

"What happened to you?" he asked as he pointed to the recently-healed scratch marks.

"Your mother and I were wrestling and she did this to me while playing," Patrick responded. Jeremiah noticed the panic look on his face as everyone laughed.

Early the next morning, there was a knock on the door. Jeremiah watched from the bedroom he shared with his siblings as his mother walked nervously to answer the front door. The mood in the atmosphere felt intense.

"Where is he?" a forceful voice asked. "Move to the side." Several men in black uniforms entered the house while others in t-shirts wearing vests followed in a straight line as they bum-rushed the house, pointing guns. Jeremiah sat on his knees in his nightshirt and underwear as the men searched rapidly through their home. Gloria was separated from her kids. A black US marshal was talking to her on the porch while the others searched for Patrick.

"Come here, ma'am! Where is he? We know he's here," one policeman stated. A big white man wearing a straw hat pulled Gloria to the side. "If you don't tell us where he is, you're going down with him," he said to her.

"Hey, what's this?" one of the policemen asked while pointing his shotgun toward the ceiling in Gloria's closet. "Get everyone out!" The policemen grabbed the children while Troy and Catherine cried in fear. Jeremiah walked confused out of his mind and terrified that his mom was about to get arrested as he listened closely to the cops.

As they all walked out the back door, all you heard was a door being kicked open. "Freeze, don't move!" Jeremiah looked up as he stepped out the back door and all he saw was a dark figure falling from the sky. Patrick had kicked out the attic window in a desperate attempt to flee the police and US marshals. Patrick jumped from the attic window, and the policemen shoved Jeremiah in the back to prevent Patrick from landing on top of him. They all fell and the policemen pushed and shoved their way to Patrick who had twisted his ankle from the high jump. Patrick had a disappointed look on his face as they cuffed him and placed him in the back of the patrol car. Jeremiah looked back and he noticed his mom being held with her hands behind her back, and the cop prepared to take her away. The big white marshal with the straw hat was standing in the house talking to the black cop Gloria was with earlier. The marshal walked over to Gloria and removed the handcuffs. "You're extremely lucky, Ms. Walker. If this cop hadn't told me that you actually spoke to him about Patrick being in the house, I was taking you to jail for hiding a fugitive."

Within minutes, the police and US marshals all left the house, and Gloria hugged her kids as if it was the first time she held them. Jeremiah was traumatized by the police rushing through their house, pointing guns at them, loud yelling, and mostly from Patrick jumping from the attic and almost landing on top of him. Jeremiah had nightmares the next couple of weeks and even experienced problems wetting the bed before he finally healed mentally. No one ever knew these things were going on at school because Gloria enforced one rule amongst many: what happened in her house stayed in her house.

Despite recent events, Gloria didn't rush to live on her own for the next two years. She dated two different guys, hoping one of them would be her king, before giving up on the dating scene. The first guy was a 5'10" dark-skinned mechanic with short hair and a clean shave. His name was Shane, and he was a former officer in the army. He lived deep in the country and even farther than Marcus's house. He lived in a mobile home for a while before inheriting his mother's home after she married her third husband and moved away. For the most part, it was a nice home. The floors creaked in certain parts of the house, but everything worked. Well, at least in the beginning.

Just like Marcus, Shane maintained a fake exterior from Jeremiah and his siblings for a long time before truth exposed itself. Over time, Shane's attitude became aggressive, and the verbal abuse started toward Troy and Jeremiah. Every morning, he would force Jeremiah and Troy out of bed to come assist him outside in the yard. He worked for his uncle next door at their shade tree mechanic shop. His uncle did a lot of transporting junk cars, so Shane mostly operated the shop alone. Instead of teaching Jeremiah and Troy the difference between the tools, he yelled and screamed at them the entire day.

"You can't do shit! Give me that! You act soft like a freaking faggot!" Shane said to Jeremiah when he couldn't hold the transmission in the air by the greasy silver chain. Jeremiah squeezed the crowbar in his hands as he fought the desire to strike Shane across the head. Kids at school harassed him with that same name, and he was tired of being called that. He never understood why, of all things, that's what people chose to call him, or why that description was often used to reference him. Jeremiah's body temperature spiked as his eyes filled with tears of anger and hatred toward Shane. He didn't allow his tears to fall, because he didn't want to appear weak.

Troy stopped coming to help at the mechanic shop to avoid the additional verbal abuse they experienced at home. Any time Shane didn't continuously operate on a vehicle, he became ill and took his frustrations out on the kids. One day he bum-rushed them as they played in the room while their mom was out. He struck them over and over and over again with an old four- foot-long, green water hose. They'd been hit with belts, shoes, cords, and even switches, but never a water hose. Troy and Catherine screamed so loud Jeremiah's ears rung for five minutes.

"All y'all do is sit in my house and play!" Shane said to them as they all cried. He turned around and walked out the bedroom door, through the kitchen which was connected, and out the back door. The kids continued to cry as they watched the bruises appear on their bodies. The bruises burned when they took a bath later that night. He laid in bed later that night after praying, thinking of how he could change things in his life. He spazzed out in anger as he discovered the things that need changed were not within his control. He couldn't stop the bullying and harassment at home or at school; he couldn't stop his mom from dating bad guys; and he couldn't fight off the demon in his head. They never said anything to their mother about that day. Jeremiah didn't want to upset his mother and her happiness. He knew how much she loved him, but he also knew she only tolerated his ways because Shane provided for them. *Where could we go?* Jeremiah thought to himself. He couldn't think of an answer as he brainstormed, but that didn't stop the thoughts of leaving.

During the springtime in that home many things came from deep within. Many consecutive nights, Jeremiah would walk into the creepy bathroom and see a wolf-spider sitting in the tub. The tub was detached from the wall, so you could see in between and almost to the ground over time. Night after night he would walk in, see a wolf-spider with those hairy legs and big eyes, and kill it. It felt like deja vu as a new spider was there each time and just as big as the last one. It got so bad Jeremiah and his siblings stopped taking baths for a while because they were frightened of the bathroom. The sink was peeling off the wall, and the toilet rocked as you sat on it. They'd rather take wash-ups in the sink rather than step a toe into that tub.

One thing was for sure, they hated living with Shane and couldn't wait to move. He wasn't a jerk all the time; he shared similar mood swings, like Gloria. Jeremiah noticed after they made trips to the store Gloria and Shane would go straight to their room and close the door. The bedroom was on the opposite end of the living room and sectioned off by a door. You could walk from the front door, through the living-room, through the kid's room, and into the back of the house. Jeremiah could sense the evil spirit in the air as the fragrance hit the tip of his nose. He followed it to the edge of Shane's bedroom door. After putting pieces together over the years, he finally accepted what he didn't want to acknowledge.

Luckily for Jeremiah, the relationship didn't last between the two, but he remained a close friend to Gloria. They dated on and off over the next few years, but a long-term committed relationship never worked out for the two. Anytime in the future Gloria needed to buy a cheap car, she'd always go to Shane for the right connections.

The next guy Gloria dated after the police incident was a mellow guy of light skin completion, with country roots, named Trevor. He lived maybe two miles from Marcus, and some of his relatives lived next door. He was forty-two years of age when they started dating. Jeremiah never learned what he did for a living, but he'd leave for several hours every day. Food wasn't always the best, but they had always had something edible. He lived a conservative lifestyle and seemed to be quite happy with his life. He loved Catherine and made sure each year she had a cake for her birthday, no matter how hard times were.

Jeremiah, Troy, and Catherine spent as much of their free time as they could next door with Trevor's younger nieces and cousins. They were a few years older than Jeremiah, but they didn't care as long as they had other kids to hang around. Samantha and Octavia, sophomores in high school, were the two they played with most times. They were funny and quite erotic. Jeremiah had a crush on Samantha and Troy had a crush on Octavia. One day they were hanging out in Samantha's room as Octavia finished her homework.

"I bet you won't come over here!" Samantha said to Jeremiah. He posed in his seat, lifted his right eyebrow, and rose slowly from his seat. They started kissing and grinding their bodies together. Jeremiah didn't know what he was doing so he mimicked what Samantha did and tried to put his own spin to it.

"What are y'all doing?" Octavia asked as she started giggling and covering her red face.

"You better get Troy," Samantha said to her as she laughed back.

"Ok, come on, Troy!" She said with a grin. Troy jumped onto the bed with Octavia and the both laughed loudly. Troy began kissing all over Octavia's blessed upper area. Troy discovered on that day that he was a breast man. Jeremiah smiled with pride as he saw his brother with his first girl. Neither were having sex, just wild kissing and grinding all over one another.

As Jeremiah and Troy left that evening, he looked up and noticed the streetlight had come on. Jeremiah and Troy both looked at each other simultaneously as they remembered their mother's instructions. "Be home before the street light comes on," she said to them before leaving home. "JEREMIAH!" Gloria yelled from the front step. Jeremiah and Troy dashed through the trail to get home. Gloria was standing in the doorway waiting, swinging her belt. "Didn't I tell y'all ass—Whop! Whop! Whop!" Gloria disciplined Troy and Jeremiah through the living room and all the way back to their room. Troy was a runner when it came to receiving a whooping, but Gloria had energy to burn on this particular evening, and there was no getting away this time. The boys cried as they received their last strike from their mother with the strength of Hercules. They laid there crying for a few additional moments and then turned on their backs and looked to the ceiling. The crying stopped and gradually turned into grins as they reflected on what happened with the girls. They turned to each other and laughed silently so their mother wouldn't hear. They both exhaled deeply in complete satisfaction before dozing off to sleep.

Chapter 9

THE BEAST WITHIN

Life was consistent with Trevor and by this point in their lives, Jeremiah was fully aware of his life and knew how to avoid disappointment. Trevor continued to treat them well, and Catherine maintained her spell on him. She became spoiled with her favorites, candy and dolls. He always held her in his lap whenever they family watched TV together. Chicken and rice was a constant meal while living with Trevor. It was affordable, and could be cooked in different ways. Sometimes Jeremiah missed the deer meat Patrick introduced him to.

As the weeks went by, Jeremiah noticed more clues about Trevor and his occupation. For several days they went to visit one of Trevor's cousins about five miles north from where they lived. His cousin lived in a blue trailer with three nice cars parked in the front yard. Each of them had big shiny rims. The kids always had to sit in the car while Trevor and Gloria went inside, except for one night Jeremiah vaguely remembered. During one of their traditional errand runs, they stopped by his cousin's house one night. There was a strong pine cone smell in the air, and a blue light shined throughout the room. The kids were placed on the couch and the adults went to the back. They didn't stay long, and Jeremiah glanced around the room to gather details about the place, but the blue light made it difficult to see clearly. The adults walked up the hallway toward them as they closed a door behind them. Trevor's cousin, a tall, heavyset guy with cornrows, continued to talk with his hand on Trevor's shoulder. All Jeremiah was able to hear through the rap music playing in the background was, "I knew you didn't steal from me!" Trevor laughed nervously as they shook hands.

Things were quiet that night as Trevor and Gloria spent most of it in the room. Due to the similar characteristics Jeremiah saw in Trevor when compared to the previous men in their lives, he became suspicious after that night. The evil spirit circled Trevor and Gloria often as Jeremiah's senses were spiked with the aroma seeping from the cracks of the bedroom. Gloria came from the back room to check on the kids as they watched Sanford and Son on television in the living room with all the lights off. Jeremiah obtained a great look at Gloria's face as the light from the floor TV reflected on her face. He exhaled softly, as he'd noticed the same stimulated eyes before. He grew depressed because this demon of hers was ruining the family. He couldn't grasp why it was so important or why every guy she dated had this evil in common. He began to wonder if it all was even a coincidence, or if it was rather a requirement. How far back did it date as being part of their family? Was it the root of the curse which covered their family? How could something that caused so much destruction remain a constant in their live no matter where they moved or how hard things became?

These questions occupied his mind every day as he persevered through their daily struggles. Jeremiah had such a spark which ignited from deep within his soul, and he fought every day to create a positive and determined atmosphere around him. Fortunately, he was attending the small high school in the country where bullying and harassment wasn't a problem. He was able to focus on his academics and being a kid once again. He joked with his buddies and flirted with the upper class high school girls although he was only in the sixth and seventh grade when he attended this school. He liked this one light-skinned girl named August. She had long black hair and was built like a volleyball player. He flirted with her any time his pals hyped him up to do so. As he stood beside her one day in the downstairs science laboratory, Jeremiah gripped her booty and stood there with a nonchalant look. August turned and looked at Jeremiah with a huge grin. She couldn't believe what Jeremiah was doing because she thought he was too shy. She reached down, grabbed his hand, and smacked it!

"Oh sorry, I didn't realize where my hand was. It was so soft!" Jeremiah responded quickly with a smirk. They laughed for a second and Jeremiah slid away smoothly while the chemistry was still strong. They flirted in between classes but never actually dated. Jeremiah knew she was out of his league, but he enjoyed the chase.

Everything seemed normal in that department until in the gym and locker room when he would see his demon come alive. Only certain specimens caused it, and Jeremiah wasn't sure how he felt about it at this point. However, Jeremiah loved the spirit of this high school. The teachers were caring and oftentimes paid for Jeremiah to participate in the class field trips. The administrative staff were strict and yet compassionate. He enjoyed every moment, while one year Jeremiah and two of his best friends scored the three highest test scores on the state exam for the county. It was a good thing Jeremiah was the type of individual to live life to the fullest in every moment, because this calmness in his life wouldn't last long. He knew his life wasn't perfect and that he was born into a life of disadvantages, but he preferred to dwell on his blessings rather than worldly desires and society's standards which sometimes caused an awful level of depression. "My life will not always be this way! I just have to keep praying for direction and guidance," Jeremiah repeated to himself frequently to remind him of the power of the Lord.

It had only been a few days since they visited Trevor's cousin that bizarre night. The hostility in the house intensified as more and more arguments broke out between Gloria and Trevor even though Christmas was only a few days away. Jeremiah already knew the deal; don't ask for anything, because it's just another day. However, Troy and Catherine shared a list with Trevor of the things they wanted for Christmas. Jeremiah grew nervous because he didn't want them to get their hopes up, but he also didn't want to kill their spirit. Jeremiah chose not to impose on the situation as the tree remained lonely day after day.

Christmas morning arrived and the kids screamed with excitement as presents were displayed neatly under the tree. The kids searched the wrapped boxes for their names and ripped the paper off in blissful happiness. The kids continued to unwrap their gifts as someone knocked on the door. A few of Trevor's relatives from next door walked in. "Someone tagged our house and stole gifts. We hate to ask, but did you take anything from our house?" they asked Trevor.

"No, I didn't steal anything from y'all. I bought these gifts myself," Trevor replied. Samantha and Octavia reached down as they recognized the wrapping paper on a few of the gifts.

"These are our gifts," the girls said as they revealed the toys. The relatives began grabbing gifts from the floor, including some the kids had already unwrapped. They shook their heads in disappointment because Trevor had robbed them before Christmas and lied to their face about it. Jeremiah's heart stopped as he stood there in disbelief. *How in the hell does this keep happening?* Jeremiah asked himself. *Time after time, tragedy creates obstacles in our life as if we're not worthy of living stress-free. Either our utilities get cut off, we're kicked out of our home, we don't have food, or we're being abused. I'm tired of the rollercoaster!*

Jeremiah was disenchanted by Trevor's decisions, but on the other hand, none of Gloria's previous boyfriends went through such lengths to ensure they had a merry Christmas. Jeremiah was concerned that Trevor would steal from his own relatives, but he also considered that Trevor figured his relatives wouldn't miss out since they always purchased a surplus of gifts. However, that still didn't make it right. Later that night, Gloria and Trevor had a heated argument that didn't end well. At first, they were just talking, and then things escalated. They exchanged words savagely as three of Trevor's cousins from next door arrived outside. The presence of his cousins increased Trevor's confidence in his argument, and his male ego superseded his normal tendency of being chivalrous toward his lady. His cousins stood behind him as he spoke disrespectfully to Gloria.

Gloria was no timid woman, so she stood her ground although she was alone. Trevor made his way to the hall closet and grabbed the big trash bags. He shoved the children's clothes into the bag and a few of Gloria's belongings. He next filled a clear plastic bin with more items and placed them by the door as they continued to argue. Trevor threatened to throw the bags of clothes outside on the ground.

"I'm telling you now, don't touch my babies' clothes. You can talk all you want in front on your kin, but don't throw our items on the ground," Gloria said to Trevor in a tone that would make Batman whimper.

"You don't tell me what the hell to do, woman, in my house," Trevor said as he grabbed two bags and tossed them outside. As Trevor opened the door to throw the bags, Gloria reached on the counter and snatched the hammer. Pow! Pow! Gloria struck Trevor once on the top of his head and the second time on his shoulder as she followed by a kick to his anus. Trevor propelled forward and fell to the ground in front of his relatives.

"I warned you not to touch our stuff, but you wanted to put on a show!" Gloria yelled as she gripped the hammer tightly by her side. Trevor left with his cousins shortly after, feeling embarrassed and shame. Gloria and her kids moved out a few days later. She always taught her kids to never stay where they aren't safe or welcomed.

Gloria managed to convince her older daughter, Olivia, to open her home to them for a few weeks until she located a new place to rent. Olivia agreed, and so they moved in for five weeks before renting a trailer of their own within the city limits. Living with their older sister was a nightmare for Jeremiah, because day after day he observed as his sister treated them like unwanted guests. Most days Olivia walked around with a disturbed look on her face; squinted eyes, wrinkled forehead, tight jaws, and pouted lips was her typical facial expression description. Jeremiah didn't fully understand, and he never asked why she behaved in such a disgusting manner. All he wanted was a nondiscriminatory household with the basic living essentials so he could finish high school and be a positive role model for his family.

Here is what Jeremiah knew for certain. He knew they had different fathers and that his sister loved her father's side of the family. Only Jeremiah, Troy, and Catherine shared the same father. He never heard Olivia speak ill of her other relatives, and she always participated in planning birthday parties and other family celebrations with her father's side. Olivia was always there when they needed her. She loved her kids and would do anything within her power to provide a better life than the one she was forced to live. Jeremiah knew Olivia worked hard for the new lifestyle she'd now grown accustomed to, but he often wondered where the younger siblings fit into her life. Jeremiah figured she must have had resentment toward their mother for the hell she put them through. After all, Gloria had proven to be irresponsible through her actions from time to time. He figured Olivia never forgave Gloria for creating the circumstances of their life that forced her to move out on her own.

However, it was never understood why Jeremiah, Troy, and Catherine always received the short end of her love and affection, when the circumstances of their life were not their fault. In Jeremiah's eyes, they were victims of the same challenges and barriers. Year after year, Jeremiah, Troy, and Catherine were lucky if they even received a happy birthday from their oldest sister, and they knew better than to ask for anything. Olivia took pride in splurging around birthdays, on school outfits, and most importantly on Christmas for her own kids. Hundreds of dollars were spent on each of her four children, but not a dime on her younger siblings who hardly ever received even a pair of socks.

Many Christmas mornings, Jeremiah and his younger siblings had to watch as their nieces and nephews opened box after box in excitement while they lived vicariously through them. Each year they hoped to hear, "This is for you, guys!" No such words ever formed from their sister's mouth. You may say she had the opposite of Nicole's generosity and thoughtfulness when the subject pertained to the younger siblings. However, Jeremiah loved Olivia just as much as Nicole. No matter her character flaws, Jeremiah would fight and protect her from anything threatening her health, safety, or happiness

Chapter 10

New Beginnings

Summer was coming to an end when Gloria and her three youngest kids moved into a trailer park on the east side of town. Life was steady for a moment. Since they didn't move far, they often saw Olivia and her kids in public. The grandkids always ran to hug their grandmother, uncles, and aunt no matter the venue. Jeremiah and the younger siblings never changed their behavior toward their older sister Olivia or her kids. Although they were disappointed in her decisions from time to time, they never judged her or held a grudge.

At the end of the day, family is family. You don't belittle family or make them feel inadequate simply because of a disagreement. In life, you learn to accept family members for who they are as individuals. If the person had a character flaw, then you did what you could to help the person better themselves. However, if a member of the family liked their space or didn't get along well with others, then you accepted it and took appropriate measures to help you deal with their preference. Even though a person may be your relative, you have no clue what mental battles the individual fights on a day-to-day basis. Materialism destroys family, friendships, and relationships, so Jeremiah and his younger siblings were not intrigued to pull their family apart for money or gifts. They just wanted their sister to know they existed and had feelings, too.

Troy and Catherine were of age now to fully understand how they were suffering and the decisions which contributed to their daily struggles. They put their childish ways behind as their teenage years were quickly approaching. More time was spent arguing and pointing the blame as the children grew older. Finally, normalcy in the household!

As the family continued to get settled into their new home, they made a trip back to Trevor's house to gather their clothes and other personal items. Since the family moved so much, they never accumulated an abundance of household items. They always started from scratch when Gloria ever rented a place of her own. Using the car Shane helped her purchase with tax money, Gloria drove her kids to the country where Trevor lived. As they arrived at his trailer late that evening, the kids noticed smoke rising in the air. Gloria decreased the speed of her red '99 Mazda.

Red and blue lights flashed repeatedly as the car maneuvered closer. There was yellow tape circling his place and cops standing everywhere. As Gloria creeped into the driveway, her headlights beamed ahead as the family noticed the figure. Strapped to the big white oak tree next to the trailer with barbed wire was Trevor, burned to a crisp! Trevor was murdered!

"Oh, my goodness! I can't believe my eyes. He didn't deserve this treatment. No one deserves to die this way!" Gloria stated out loud as she placed the car in park and cried in the arms of Jeremiah. The smoke from his burnt body continued to rise as the smell of human flesh seeped into their nostrils.

Jeremiah gazed at the flashing lights of the police car until he fell into a daze, spiritless. The last time they saw Trevor was the night of the argument between him and their mother. Jeremiah always wondered if the murder was connected to the night they visited Trevor's cousin's house that smelled like pine cones. Jeremiah could still visualize that night and the tone of the big guy who placed his hand on Trevor's shoulder.

The family was completely distraught on their ride home, as they'd just seen their first dead body together of someone they knew closely. The family returned home depressed because Trevor held a very special place in each of their hearts. Aside from the night he threw their clothes outside and told them to leave when having an argument with Gloria, he always gave his all to provide for them. He always made the kids feel special, and he spent time teaching Jeremiah and Troy to be a man instead of bullying them like Shane. The kids didn't dwell on Shane kicking them out, because Gloria emphasized the importance of leaning and depending on God and not man.

Gloria sowed many seeds of wisdom in her young kids to ensure they'd thrive as they grew older and entered the real world. No, her kids didn't receive the best shoes, and yes, they moved regularly, but they were never short of a loving and nurturing mother. The life obstacles they overcame would one day pay off significantly for the driven children in the long run. The two things you can't beat in life are experience and exposure!

Over the next year, the family focused on living their best life. Troy and Catherine were gearing up for middle school and Jeremiah faced the pressure of entering high school. The trailer park wasn't as bad as they originally expected it to be. They were expecting frequent gun shots, burglaries, and domestic violence. However, the most annoying thing they experienced were the loud cars, neighborhood gossip, and annoyingly intrusive neighborhood kids.

Jeremiah, Troy, and Catherine loved one thing about this new environment; the candy lady! They never knew her name, so they just called her the candy lady. She had all the best snack cakes, chocolate bars, chewy candy, chips, and even Kool-Aid freeze cups! Jeremiah remembered freeze cups from when they lived in the city. They often walked the neighborhood throughout the summer to learn more about the community and available walking paths.

One day, Troy was approached by another kid who was slightly bigger than him. "What are you doing around here?" the kid asked.

"I'm just taking a walk," Troy replied.

"Well, you need to find another path to reach your destination, because this is my street, and no one crosses unless I give them permission, punk!"

Troy stood there with a confused look on his face, wondering if the situation was a prank.

"Dude move out of my way!" Troy said to the tall teenager as he tried to walk by. The teenager shoved Troy to the ground and Jeremiah sprinted to his assistance.

"Don't you ever put your hands on my brother," Jeremiah said to the bully as he helped his brother up.

The teenager took two steps back and began walking away after listening to the tone of Jeremiah's voice. As he turned around, he made a snarky comment at Jeremiah. Jeremiah took another step forward. "Don't be walking behind me," the teenager said forcefully.

"You better leave my brother alone, and that's all I know," said Jeremiah. The guy turned around quickly and punched Jeremiah in the face. What the teenager didn't know was that Jeremiah fought all the time when they lived in the harsh projects of the city, so he could take a punch.

With the might of Zeus, Jeremiah slapped fire from the teenager. POW! It was the loudest slap Troy and Catherine had ever heard! The sound echoed through the street as the teenager held his face while tears formed in his eyes. When he removed his hand, Troy and Catherine saw their big brother's hand print in the guy's face.

"Damn!" Troy and Catherine said at the same time as they began to laugh. The teenager continued to walk away, and he never bothered Troy again. Jeremiah felt like a hero for protecting his brother and defending his integrity. He was placed in this uncomfortable situation time after time throughout his childhood, but Gloria always taught that while living in the projects, if one- person fights, everyone fights.

Jeremiah wasn't into violence, but when provoked, he didn't hesitate to protect his family. A similar issue, but on a bigger scale, occurred during their last trip of the summer. Nicole and her boyfriend Jeremy came to pick up Jeremiah, Troy, and Catherine the week before school started. This was perfect timing, because the kids thought they would end another summer break without even leaving the town where they resided. A vacation for the kids and a break for mommy was exactly what the family needed, but the drama associated with the trip wasn't expected. Jeremiah never saw this one coming.

Chapter 11

THE SELFLESS SOUL

The vacation didn't go as planned. Nicole and Jeremy had an altercation. Jeremiah, Troy, and Catherine were in the house while Nicole and Jeremy made a quick trip to the store to buy groceries. Catherine heard tires screeching and jolted toward the door to look.

"Oh, no! Jeremiah!" Catherine said frantically. Jeremiah and Troy loped quickly toward her. They watched as Jeremy's car came to a stop in the middle of the road. Jeremy's teenage nieces and aunt from next door rushed out of their houses.

Jeremiah, Troy, and Catherine walked slowly to see what everyone was watching. As they walked closer, they shockingly realized Jeremy was attacking their sister. Jeremiah looked at Jeremy's family members with a desperate look. He stood there and wondered why none of them would intervene. They just stood there and watched. "I have to do something," Jeremiah said to himself as he ran back into the house. He grabbed a black-handled steak knife from the kitchen and sprinted back outside.

Jeremy's relatives all ran toward Jeremiah with frightened eyes and extended arms as they yelled, "No! Wait! Don't do it!" They wrestled Jeremiah to the ground to rip the knife from his mighty grip. They weren't brave enough to stop a man from hitting a woman, but they dared to stop Jeremiah from stepping in for his sister. Jeremiah couldn't believe the audacity of these people and thought of handing out punches to each of them for being cowards and standbys.

Jeremiah thought of how muscular Jeremy was and that he kept a gun on him always. He swallowed his saliva, took a deep breath, and ran to the car at the edge of the road in front of the house. Jeremy and Nicole were still rumbling around inside the vehicle. "Get off my sister," Jeremiah said as he pushed Jeremy. Jeremy looked up as he tried to restrain Nicole and said, "Get back, boy!" He looked him in the eyes, and all Jeremiah saw were the eyes of the devil as Jeremy appeared to have no soul. Jeremiah shuffled two steps back for a second and a half, then leaned forward with all his strength and punched Jeremy in the middle of his forehead. "I said, get off my sister!"

Jeremy was on top of Nicole and tried to crawl out of the passenger window like a raging animal trying to reach Jeremiah. Jeremiah took a step back from the car and held both of his fists up in front of his face. His heart was racing beyond control, but he was prepared to fight for his sister's honor. He knew there was no way he could win, but that wasn't going to stop him from demonstrating the definition of a real man for his siblings who were witnessing this moment. Jeremiah was more afraid of his siblings being disappointed in him for not stepping-in.

"I'll kill you, punk!" Jeremy said to Jeremiah when he couldn't make it through the window. He exchanged another blow with Nicole before crawling out the driver's door. He reached and grabbed the plastic crate from the back seat and attempted to hit Nicole, but it was blocked by the seat on each attempt. He slammed the door in frustration and walked angrily down the street. Nicole parked the car in the front yard. Within sixty seconds, she had flattened all the tires, burst all the windows, and poured oil into the gas tank.

Jeremiah had seen them argue before, but never witnessed them take it to the point where they fought like MMA fighters. He recalled them shoveling each other around the house before when Nicole slammed him on the bathroom sink. She was a strong young woman like her mother, and her bite was much worse than her bark.

A year went by and nothing seemed to get better for the family. Gloria's car was totaled after a deer jumped in front of her car, she was laid off from her job, her habit kicked in strong, and bills turned into late payment notices. You could feel the tension in the air as the new school year approached. The kids started sorting through their clothes to find the best outfits for the first week of school. Jeremiah was now heading to ninth grade; meanwhile, Troy and Catherine were excited about middle school.

Over the summer, Jeremiah battled a major life decision along with the other chaos in his life. He didn't want to attend the city high school with the same kids from his middle school or the older kids who were ahead of him. Jeremiah had stupendous goals and aspirations for his future. There was nothing he wanted more than to attend college on a full scholarship. He knew that since he was poor, he only had three reasonable options. 1. Prepare to join the military. 2. Go to college on a full academic scholarship. 3. Stay around town, become like his surroundings, and influence his siblings to do the same by his lack of effort.

He knew if he attended the city high school he wouldn't finish school with a clean record. The bullying and harassment he endured in middle school wasn't part of his plan for high school, and his temperament was spiraling out of control. Jeremiah was serious about his education, and he just felt himself on the edge of snapping considering the never-ending trials of his life. Rage was building inside of Jeremiah, and he didn't want the darkness to get the best of him.

Troy and Catherine deserved to see their big brother grow up and achieve his dreams. They deserved to have a positive role model implementing positive change in their lives. They were worthy of knowing the joys of success and that they were invaluable. Jeremiah simply wanted them to have all the happiness in the world, and whatever their definition of happiness meant was fine with him.

Although he wanted to accomplish this goal for them, he didn't want his siblings to feel abandoned by him. Jeremiah was contemplating moving out. He knew life wouldn't be any easier, but breaking the curse that covered his family for decades had to be broken. *Someone has to step up, face their fears, and do what hasn't been done before to build a solid path for the rest!* These were the final thoughts Jeremiah said to himself before walking into his mother's room to have the hardest discussion of his adolescent life.

He remembered his mother speaking of moving back in with one of her exes since things fell so far out of hand with the bills and rent. Jeremiah figured this was as good as it would get for timing. He walked into Gloria's room and explained to her why he couldn't move back in with her ex and attend the city school. Jeremiah was quite skilled at articulating his thoughts in an affectionate manner. He didn't want his mom to think it had anything to with her, but that the smaller high school in the country would be more conducive for his education and future.

Jeremiah knew the bigger high school was receiving more money than the smaller high school because they were in different divisions with better buses, one school's athletics teams had multiple jerseys in each sport, and the architecture of both schools were on different platforms. He also wondered if both schools received the same quality of teachers, or if one school was favored more than the other. Even with all of this on his mind, Jeremiah was willing to live with his decision because he was determined to be an educated, successful, and influential role model for his family.

Jeremiah knew that for Troy and Catherine to believe he still wanted to be a part of their lives, he had to show them. Jeremiah never desired to be like the other men who invaded their lives, and he was determined to show them how much he loved them through his actions and not words. Jeremiah didn't want to miss all the dialogue, laughs, face-to-face mentoring, and adventures of living with his siblings. *Can I really do this on my own, Lord?* Jeremiah would ask with his heart trembling in self-doubt. Dreaming of a master plan was one thing, but to embark on the journey with nothing but hope could be terrifying for a young adolescent. "This is so much bigger than me. It's not actually about me. No one has ever made sacrifices for us, but I'm willing to do it for them!" Jeremiah spoke his final words of empowerment into existence.

Chapter 12

It's Not Over

When times are hard, and the night hour seems to never end, it's important to be connected to an impenetrable source of power, so that your faith won't waver. Since the day he learned about his name, Jeremiah's life had been intertwined with the Bible, and this connection would be a fence against the dark forces along his journey. He was confident that if God protected and carried him through the obstacles of his past, the Lord would surely secure a path for his future. Jeremiah knew that in order for his dreams to become a reality, he had to put forth effort. His mother used to tell him, "Baby you have to work and pray! If you're going to ask the Lord for something, then be willing to give something and make sacrifices."

Jeremiah thought about his mother's words as he worked tirelessly to obtain his high school diploma. He knew he was making a strenuous sacrifice by leaving home, but he knew there was a purpose for his life. Jeremiah didn't quite know what his purpose was, but he was willing to travel to the end of the earth and battle any demon to discover his truth.

The next four years of high school were hell for Jeremiah, but he remained thankful for all those Sundays his mother made him go to church. He bounced from home to home over the next four years facing manipulating adults who would take advantage of his vulnerability, conniving teenagers who would betray his trust, and emotionally disconnected relatives who couldn't identify his suffering. Despite the trauma in his life, Jeremiah fought to be a man of his word because he made a promise to his mom, Troy, and Catherine.

Every summer after the school year ended, Jeremiah competed for and excelled in academic summer programs offered at the local universities. The programs were intense, but Jeremiah fell more in love with the idea of attending college. Living on campus with the other students had an astounding impact on his life.

Each program awarded the participants with a stipend. Jeremiah used the money from his summer programs to purchase school supplies, clothes, shoes, and personal items for Troy and Catherine. He didn't want them to experience what he went through, so Jeremiah used the skills God blessed him with to make a difference. He enjoyed making them happy, and seeing the smiles on their faces made his sacrifices seem worthwhile. All Jeremiah wanted was for them to be happy and live as little kids should, without worries or adult responsibilities.

He worked many side jobs throughout high school no matter where he moved to help his mom pay rent and utilities. He worked with carpenters, on a chicken farm, on landscaping projects, and even babysitting. He did his best to help Troy and Catherine with their needs as he worked desperately in between sports.

For every trial he faced, Jeremiah embarked on a new task that would benefit his future. Thanks to the help of his teachers and coaches, Jeremiah participated in many varsity sport teams, leadership organizations, and even served as the senior class president. For once, being poor didn't hinder him from participating in simple activities.

Jeremiah worked ridiculously hard to suppress the negativity in his life. For the first three years, he managed to keep his personal struggles a secret. No one was aware he wasn't living at home with his mom. He truly learned the skill of separating his personal life from school because his mother always said, "what happens in my house stays in my house.

He was never fond of the spotlight on his personal life. Jeremiah confided in one of the school's staff members once, but the adult manipulated him, twisted his words, and used his pain to benefit herself and framed it as a benefit for others. Even through his childhood, he never had sleepovers at his house with classmates, so no one ever saw the conditions he endured or the pain he learned to disguise so well. Now he was out on his own trying to make a way to the finish line and across the graduation stage, but the expedition would be a bumpy ride.

The first home he lived in was with the Smiths. The Smiths were a military house with strict rules in a beautiful five-bed, two-bath family home. Jeremiah and their one and only son spent every evening and early morning cleaning the house. Mopping, sweeping, clearing gutters, cutting grass, trimming hedges, dusting, and anything in between that could be cleaned every day, starting at four forty-five in the morning.

Jeremiah wasn't new to cleaning because Gloria never allowed a filthy house, but the constant demands of the family were overbearing considering sport activities, homework, side jobs, and other extracurricular activities. The father spoke to him rudely and eventually kicked him out for being disrespectful. Jeremiah fought his anger as Mr. Smith often verbally abused him.

"You're not my father! I didn't ask for someone to replace my father; I just asked for a place to live!" Jeremiah said as he slammed the door during his exit from the house after their final argument.

He asked one of his fellow teammates on the football team if he could live with them for a while. His teammate had three other siblings who were also in high school. Jeremiah hated living with the family because it was full of violence. The mother and father argued all the time, two of the brothers fought all the time, and Jeremiah was shown no respect. The family rarely cooked, so most times they were on their own for food. Scraping money from his savings and periodically asking his football coaches for money, Jeremiah managed to not to perish.

Two of the siblings did the unthinkable and belittled Jeremiah in front of a group of students by exposing and discussing the details of his private life. They talked about him being homeless and always wearing the same clothes. They made jokes about him not having name-brand clothes and often accused him of being gay. Jeremiah couldn't comprehend how anyone could be so cruel. Drowning in anger, depression, and doubt, Jeremiah laid many nights in silence as the fire inside became dimmer and the feeling of hopelessness and being voiceless suppressed him into a dark place.

Jeremiah was tired of the negative energy that continued to take over his life. He bounced from to home-to-home, was treated like dirt, and still faced harassment in school. *I don't know if I can pull this off, Lord,* Jeremiah would say to himself many dark nights as he cried himself to sleep. He did his best to offset the harassment by allowing people to get to know his personality. Jeremiah was smart and used football practice as a time to handle those who spoke harshly about him instead of fighting and facing suspension. Round after round, Jeremiah would pound the guys into the ground, and it earned him the starting linebacker position.

He joked around with the jocks and thug types to demonstrate he was more than the poor smart kid who always completed his homework. He played animated card games with the nerds. Jeremiah even spent countless hours with his classmates studying for high school graduation exams when they became seniors. Jeremiah wanted to display who God created him to be as opposed to what the rumors or comments implied by insecure teenagers.

As you could imagine, Jeremiah was serious about graduating, but he was also passionate about helping others achieve their goals. As the senior class president, Jeremiah took advantage of his position to make an impact, despite the way his classmates bickered behind his back. They called him names, mocked him because of his ambition, and talked about how he dressed.

However, Jeremiah still organized study groups because he didn't want anyone to fail. This passion to assist others to live a prosperous life lead Jeremiah to convincing two students from dropping out.

"You are beautiful, smart, and deserving of happiness. Now, you live for more than just yourself. You have to do this for your child," Jeremiah said to one female student as she cried in his arms minutes after he convinced her not to leave or to give up on her education.

As the class president, he noticed that many members of his class were not as financially stable as the appearance they were presenting. He worked with the executive committee to organize fish fries, parties, car washes, donut sales, and even instituted parking fees at home sport games. Each student could withdraw from the class account with approval of the president to pay for their senior dues and prom fees. The only requirement was that each student must participate in the fundraising activities to make a withdrawal.

Well, it was finally three weeks from graduation, and Jeremiah was a nervous wreck because all his dreams were falling into place. Despite the turmoil and trauma, Jeremiah maintained a 4.0 grade point average and earned the title of class valedictorian. He received eight football scholarship offers and eight academic scholarship offers from schools all over the country. Jeremiah was even admitted into an early summer program that allowed him to start college immediately after the program ended. Nothing could ruin his happiness, or at least he thought.

Jeremiah received a random call from his father two weeks before graduation. "I miss you, son! I'm very proud of you and I just want you to know I'm coming to watch you graduate! I wouldn't miss it for anything in the world." Jeremiah still had heartburn from his father abandoning him. Although he had a wall built to protect his heart from being broken again, hearing those words from his father rung in his ears every day. *Why would he appear in my life so late? Why, after more than fifteen years, did he return?* These are questions Jeremiah asked himself.

The day finally arrived, and Jeremiah knew this would be the most memorable day of his life. His speech was prepared and all he thought about was the promise his father made. In Jeremiah's eyes, there was no pain like the sting of disappointment by someone you loved.

Throughout his middle and high school years, Jeremiah didn't have his relatives in attendance at his award shows. Dozens of ceremonies recognized Jeremiah for his incomparable accolades, but his parents and older siblings were never there to support him. Living in poverty with a single mother who was overtaken by her inner demons and having a deadbeat father forced him to concentrate on his core values and how they could be utilized to make a difference in the lives of those around him who suffered. With them both being strung out on their demons, there was no room for failure or excuses.

Exhausted by all the responsibility he accepted early in his life, Jeremiah grew eager to move away and spend some time discovering more about himself and the personal issues he'd neglected over the years. He just felt it would be better to stay focused on his family and goals rather than throw himself a pity party. He wasn't privileged with the time to dwell on such emotions. Jeremiah never quite dealt with the anger buried deep from the heartburn caused by those who bullied him. He never stopped to ponder on the discomfort he experienced from those attempting to treat him like a charity case. Even in the years his father spent absent from his life, he never cursed his name or blamed his father for their shortcomings.

Considering the verbal and physical abuse, neglect, bullying, and all the negative influences in his life, Jeremiah could have taken the easy road and just given up. The patience, maturity, faith, and self-discipline that was required to prevent him from becoming a statistic could have easily made a normal kid snap. Jeremiah was one bad decision away from converting to another angry, violent, non-goal-setting teenager with no developed skills or future. Some kids were simply destined for greatness, and Jeremiah was determined to be in that number.

It didn't matter to Jeremiah; he would go to the end of the earth to live his purpose, even if that meant studying eight consecutive weeks without any TV, entertainment, or socializing just to prepare for college entry exams. There was something special about Jeremiah, and despite how some may have felt about him, you couldn't deny his hard work and dedication to become a testimony for others to be empowered by to chase their dreams. He wanted to be a difference in his family and community, and one day he knew his day would come.

Glaring across the field and standing in front of the crowd of hundreds, Jeremiah delivered his valedictorian speech to his senior class. The audience laughed and some even cried as he poured his heart out in a humorous manner. Jeremiah could feel the cool sensation start from his heart and spread throughout his body as his speech influenced the crowd. He never saw Troy or Catherine smile with such admiration. In his speech, Jeremiah recognized many people who made a profound mark on his life, and he also challenged his classmates to inspire others as they pursued happiness. The crowd gave a standing ovation as he concluded. On that evening, Jeremiah felt something deep within. He felt his voice for the first time! He felt the source of his power of influence!

After the ceremony, one of Jeremiah's classmates walked up to him with teary eyes and stated, "Man, I never would have been able to do this without you. It's because of you I'm here today, and one day I'm going to tell my kids you're the guy who helped me earn my diploma." It was one of many thoughts that flooded his mind later that night and into the next day as he traveled to college to enroll in his summer program.

Despite the positivity that surrounded him, Jeremiah felt heartbroken by the disappointment of his father not showing up. *Why would he lie? Why make empty promises after being absent for more than fifteen years? Why cause me more pain? Why ruin my one special day?* It appeared the emotional rollercoaster that clouded his life was not yet over.

Jeremiah's mind zoned out as the sun shined brightly across his chocolate skin on the bus heading north to his destiny. College was all he ever dreamed about, and now the time had come to truly test his discipline, faith, and perseverance.

After an hour of sunbathing on the bus with musical tunes dancing in his ear, the beautiful scenery captivated his mind and a smile swept across his face as he grew fascinated with the thoughts of being free. "I feel liberated, and one day, I'll truly figure out who I am," Jeremiah whispered to himself as he inhaled and exhaled deeply and slowly while the sun beamed on his face. He didn't know what battles were ahead of him, but Jeremiah chose to walk by faith and not by sight.

Jeremiah kept repeating to himself, "I am somebody. I will be somebody. Because I am somebody!"

The end...

CPSIA information can be obtained
at www.ICGtesting.com
Printed in the USA
LVHW080804160720
660378LV00007B/115